Windows to the Past

The Town of Jackson (looking southeast toward Cache Creek), c. 1910. Photo by S. N. Leek (BC.0403). S. N. Leek Collection, American Heritage Center, University of Wyoming.

Windows to the Past

Early Settlers in Jackson Hole

by
Bonnie Kreps

Foreword by
Sherry L. Smith
Professor of History
Southern Methodist University

Jackson Hole
Historical Society
& Museum

JACKSON, WYOMING
2006

Published by
Jackson Hole Historical Society and Museum
P. O. Box 1005
Jackson, Wyoming 83001
(307) 733-9605
www.jacksonholehistory.org

Editorial Review: Sigrid Asmus
Cover and book design: Rebecca Woods
Cover photograph: Si Ferrin's boys—Bob, Merritt, and Harvey, n.d. Jackson Hole Historical Society and Museum, Gift of the Ferrin family, 2005.0153.003.
Author photo by Thomas D. Mangelson

ISBN-13   978-1-886402-06-5
ISBN-10   1-886402-06-X

Library of Congress Cataloging-in-Publication Data

Kreps, Bonnie.
Windows to the Past : Early Settlers in Jackson Hole/by Bonnie Kreps;
with foreword by Sherry L. Smith.
        p. cm.
Summary: "Explores the lives, hardships, and successes of ten families
that homesteaded in Jackson Hole, Wyoming during the late nineteenth and
early twentieth centuries. Drawn from primary source material for local
history including oral histories, family histories, and other local
records"—Provided by publisher.
Includes bibliographical references and index.
ISBN-13: 978-1-886402-06-5 (pbk. : alk. paper)
ISBN-10: 1-886402-06-X (pbk. : alk. paper)
 1. Jackson Hole (Wyo.)—History—19th century. 2. Jackson Hole
(Wyo.)—History—20th century. 3. Pioneers—Wyoming—Jackson
Hole—Biography. 4. Jackson Hole (Wyo.)—Biography. 5. Frontier and
pioneer life—Wyoming—Jackson Hole. 6. Jackson Hole (Wyo.)—Social life
and customs. I. Jackson Hole Historical Society and Museum. II. Title.
F767.T28K74 2006
978.7'55—dc22
                                2006014590

WITH THANKS

The publication of this book was made possible through the generosity of the following supporters.

Latham Jenkins/Circummero Stock Agency

The Community Foundation of Jackson Hole

Fighting Bear Antiques
Terry Winchell and Claudia Bonnist

Carter Gray

The Norman Hirschfield Foundation

The Lynne Cheney Charitable Fund
of the Community Foundation of Jackson Hole

Old Bill's Fun Run
of the Community Foundation of Jackson Hole

Rebecca Woods/White Willow Publishing

The Wyoming Council for the Humanities

ACKNOWLEDGMENTS

Many people were helpful as I researched and wrote this book, and I am grateful to them all. First of all, I thank my mother, Inger Koedt, who had the idea that I should write the book. She read and commented on my chapters as I wrote them. Stephen Lottridge, Robert Righter, and Sherry Smith served as humanities scholars on this book. I thank them for their input. Anne Koedt and Ellen Levine gave me useful early editorial ideas. John Daugherty's book, *A Place Called Jackson Hole*, was an invaluable resource; his meticulous research into primary sources provided a solid basis of fact on which I based my own research. My research was also aided by the staff of the Jackson Hole Historical Society and Museum; by the staff of Teton County Library; and by Grand Teton National Park Historian, Pam Holtman. Sherry L. Daigle and the staff of the Teton County Clerk's Land Records Office provided research assistance and legal documents when I was stumped.

Members and friends of the ten families I wrote about were available for interviews, some of them several times. They also offered essential photographs for the book. Without their generosity, the book would lack a vital element. Thank you Cliff and Martha Hansen, Bob and Jane Kranenberg, Bob and Pat Dornan, Dave Dornan, Reade Dornan, Dave Edmiston, Tom and Ruth Lindley, Rod Newcomb, Herb and Quita Pownall, and John and Marjorie Ryan.

The majority of photographs in the book are from the archives of the Jackson Hole Historical Society and Museum—thank you, Karen de Caussin, for going through hundreds of photographs with me, and for creating order and sanity. Hart Photography in Idaho Falls, Planet Jackson Hole (www.planetjh.com), Grand Teton National Park, the Jackson Hole News and Guide, Bill Koopman, and Brad Moulton all generously donated their photographs. Thanks also go to Richard Collier and Cindy L. Brown at the Wyoming State Historic Preservation Office for their ready help in searching for photographs. CameraAmerica in Jackson scanned dozens of photographs—everything from tiny old, faded ones to large ones encased in fancy frames—and generally performed miracles.

Throughout the entire book process, Lokey Lytjen, Executive Director of the Jackson Hole Historical Society and Museum, was a fine partner. I thank her for her hard work and for her sense of humor. Preparing a final manuscript for publication is a task filled with tedious but necessary details. Here, again, Karen de Caussin was a wonderful partner. She helped keep my frustration within bounds, for which I thank her most warmly. I also thank historian Sherry Smith for some lively discussions, for writing the foreword to the book, and for the pleasure of working with her, and Sigrid Asmus for her editorial review.

The research and writing of this book was made possible through a generous grant from the Wyoming Council for the Humanities and through the Old Bill's Fun Run of the Community Foundation of Jackson Hole. I greatly appreciate their support, as does the Jackson Hole Historical Society and Museum. Thank you.

—Bonnie Kreps

Covered wagon in Jackson Hole, 1913. Jackson Hole Historical Society and Museum, Schofield Collection, BC.0012.

CONTENTS

USING ORAL HISTORY

⊰⊶⊶⊶○⊷⊷⊷⊱

What is oral history? It is the experiences, remembrances, and stories of people in a family, neighborhood or community that are passed on orally. This type of history captures the contemporary knowledge of individuals gleaned from firsthand experience of events or places on audio or video media, and preserves this information for generations to come.

In documenting local history, such as the stories of a family or a community, the traditional historical sources may be limited or may not provide vivid or comprehensive pictures of the past. In situations like this, oral histories provide an excellent way to discover additional information about local history. During the researching and writing of this book, *Windows to the Past: Early Settlers in Jackson Hole*, oral narratives and family histories provided a tool that was invaluable in painting the picture of the earliest settlements in Jackson Hole.

What makes oral history particularly valuable is its capacity for finding out things that are not available in other ways. Through oral histories, one can document what people did in an ordinary day, from their work life and leisure activities to what they wore and what they ate. More importantly, one can learn how people perceived or understood the past and if their perspectives have changed over time. Oral history interviews create a personal narrative about events, places, and people. They provide the narrator with a sense of how his or her own experiences fit into a larger context. When well researched, properly conducted, and carefully examined, oral history interviews contribute uniquely to the body of knowledge about history, from the local to the national level. Carefully gathered oral history is often just as important as more traditional evidence, and this is particularly so in the case of local history.

How do you know if the information in an oral history is true? Like most other historical sources, oral histories have their strengths and weaknesses. Seldom is historic evidence absolutely accurate. Because an oral interview records an individual's life story, or chronicles events or places the narrator experienced, personal bias often enters into the narrative. The subject's memory, like those of most people, may lapse, have errors, or develop distortions over time. Bias and other weaknesses, however, are also found in more traditional historical materials. As when working with historical sources in general, one must evaluate the source and substance of oral histories and corroborate the information, to the extent possible, with a variety of materials.

Despite their limitations, oral histories may often be the only source of information available, particularly in the case of local, community, and family history. They are very important, then, in providing information about topics for which little other data exists. Oral history interviews are firsthand accounts of the experiences of particular individuals, and can shed light on many topics. When oral histories are gathered from a variety of people who witnessed events or are connected to a topic, knowledge of the subject expands significantly. Multiple narrations also enhance our understanding of the various viewpoints related to the topic and foster critical assessment of the interviews as historical data.

In working to create a useful and interesting oral history, the first step is to identify a focus or a topic to study—such as your family's history. Secondly, conduct preliminary research that will provide the basis for developing interview outlines and questions for the various narrators or speakers that you wish to interview. Having good equipment and a quiet location for conducting your interview is helpful. Careful preparation yields high-quality, rewarding interviews. Finally, making the results of your oral history project available to local libraries or archives—or to your family members—is also important.

Oral history projects are rich and rewarding ones that help future generations understand life in a bygone time and place. Much of the knowledge and understanding of the daily lives of the settlers chronicled in this book, and their direct and indirect comments about their aspirations and the challenges they faced, is derived from oral narratives about their lives. Oral histories help to balance and to expand more traditional historical resources. They reveal the personal meanings of people's lives and the lives of those around them. Moreover, the stories they uncover capture the richness of the human experience and preserve it for those who come after us—whether professional historians or those simply interested in the progression of life.

Windows to the Past: Early Settlers in Jackson Hole delves into the history of the families that shaped the Jackson Hole valley in the Northern Rockies around the turn of the nineteenth century. Stories about the family members that give color and character to the book were often drawn from family or oral histories. The Jackson Hole Historical Society and Museum hopes this book will inspire you to become interested in your own family history and traditions. For more information about oral histories and how you can document your family history, please visit the museum website, *www.jacksonholehistory.org*.

Lokey Lytjen
Executive Director
Jackson Hole Historical Society
and Museum

FOREWORD

Overshadowed as they are by the landscape's grandeur, the old historic buildings of Jackson Hole can easily be overlooked. That would be too bad, because these structures are silent witnesses to a past whose stories are quickly passing out of memory. This delightful book remedies that. It takes us inside these ruins, some over a century old, reinhabits them with the people who once lived in or used them, and preserves their stories for present and future audiences.

Human beings have long been drawn to this special patch of the American West. This book focuses on the relatively short-lived era of homesteaders—families and individuals who came to Jackson Hole from the 1890s through the 1920s, pinning their hopes on free land offered by the United States government and making a living through agriculture or, in some cases, through the budding tourist industry.

For over ten thousand years, human beings migrated into this valley searching for sustenance, but they did not settle permanently until the last century. Archaeological investigations indicate that the search for edible and medical plants attracted Jackson Hole's earliest residents, who came in the spring, followed the ripening plants to higher elevations, and moved out of the valley as fall settled in. Of course, they also hunted wild animals and some, including the Shoshone, constructed semicircular stone enclosures in the Teton and Gros Ventre Ranges, where individuals sought access to the spirit world. But the rigors of winter discouraged Indians from staying year-round.

Interestingly, the same economic and religious motives attracted Europeans and Anglo-Americans to Jackson Hole. After the federal government ushered Indians onto reservations far from the Tetons, it offered the valley's supposedly arable land to prospective farmers and ranchers through the Homestead Act of 1862. The Hansen, Shive, Ferrin, and Feuz families were among those who took advantage of these policies and moved into northwest Wyoming. In some cases the Church of Latter Day Saints (LDS or Mormon Church), headquartered in Salt Lake City, provided additional incentive to come West. Perhaps no better symbol of this religious community's powerful presence exists than the cabins nestled in close proximity to one another along "Mormon Row" in what is now Grand Teton National Park.

What links all the families featured here is the prospect of making a fresh start—the chance to own property, perhaps for the first time. Their timing was perfect. As the nation moved into the twentieth century it clung to its recent frontier past by encouraging a last gasp at homesteading. The original Homestead Act of 1862 offered 160 acres for free. In exchange homesteaders promised to settle on the land for at least five years and transform it into farmland. Most readers probably associate homesteading with the nineteenth century. For the West's high plains and more isolated spots such as Jackson Hole, however, this process had its heyday in the early decades of the 1900s.

The government's plan to encourage agriculture did not work so well in places like Jackson Hole, with its arid climate, pitifully short growing season, and rocky soil. In time Congress responded with various alterations to its original plan—the Stockgrowers Homestead Act, the Desert Land Act, the Enlarged Homestead Act, and so on—which offered concessions to Western realities, including more acreage and support for irrigation projects. Most of the people profiled here paid close attention to these offers and took advantage of them.

But something else also set Jackson Hole apart from other corners of the West: the spectacular Teton Range. Early in the twentieth century, some enterprising individuals understood the tourist potential of this place and took out homesteads for the purpose of establishing dude ranches. This was not the intention of the government, but officials allowed it anyway. The Burts, Gabbeys, and Toppings represent this approach to "homesteading." A few women, such as Geraldine Lucas and Evelyn Dornan, had no commercial designs on their homesteads but clearly filed on their particular properties for their aesthetic rather than agricultural prospects. Their descendants eventually profited from these women's wise choices.

Meanwhile, in 1929, Congress created the first incarnation of Grand Teton National Park, consisting primarily of the mountains. This move signaled several things. First, the government was no longer committed to wholesale transformation of public lands into private property. Further, it became increasingly clear that the future of the valley floor rested more with tourists than cows. Some of the families profiled here succumbed to pressures to sell their land to the park. Others held out and continued to run cattle in Jackson Hole at the turn of the millennium. But the future is now unmistakable: The homestead era is long over, and ranching is fast becoming a thing of the past.

This book takes you into the hearths and hearts of some of Jackson Hole's most interesting and compelling early-twentieth-century families. It deepens our understanding of what these people imagined the place could be, and how hard they worked to shape it into their image. Some succeeded beyond their expectations. Others eventually retreated.

These are stories of affirmation. The author's informants occasionally crack the door open onto the difficulties—the endless, bone-wearying work, the challenges of isolation, the frigid winters, the inevitable family tensions and disappointments—but for the most part, they choose to emphasize the positive. What the stories that follow make clear is that this distinctive history, despite its brevity, is well-worth remembering.

Sherry L. Smith
Professor of History
Southern Methodist University

MAP OF JACKSON HOLE

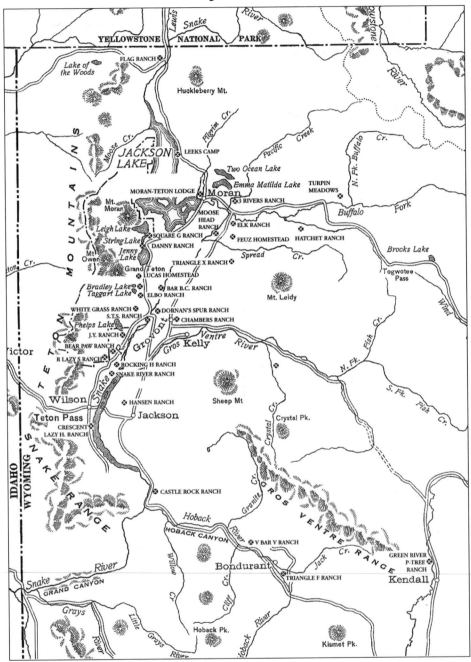

The above map has been slightly altered from its 1928 original to show homestead sites in Jackson Hole. Courtesy of the Union Pacific Railroad Museum, Union Pacific Historical Collection.

THE SETTLERS

Settlers introduction photo: Homestead families traveled to Jackson Hole in covered wagons and on horses. They carried their belongings with them, including household items, clothing, tools and equipment, cattle, and horses. Jackson Hole Historical Society and Museum, Schofield Collection, BC.0006.

CHAPTER ONE

THE SHIVE FAMILY

ARRIVED IN JACKSON HOLE IN 1891

B Y the time he homesteaded in Jackson Hole, John Shive, nick- named Jack, had already led quite an adventurous life. He was born in 1862 on a farm near Philadelphia. His father was cruel, so Jack ran away from home. At age fourteen, he was fending for himself. When he was twenty-four, he joined the army in New York City and was sent to Montana with the First Cavalry Regiment, where he took part in several clashes with the Crow. His next assignment was more peaceful. He served in Yellowstone, where he helped stock Shoshone and Yellowstone Lakes with Mackinaw trout. He left the army in 1891 and wintered in a small cabin he built for himself on the Snake River near present-day Flagg Ranch. But the willow flats of Buffalo Valley in nearby Jackson Hole drew him, and Jack Shive was one of the first set- tlers to take up land there. He built his homestead cabin near what is now the Hatchet Resort.

One of the ways settlers could homestead was by exercising squat- ter's rights, and that is how Jack acquired his first 160 acres. Squatter's rights allowed him to take up a homestead on land that not been sur- veyed. He could legally mark off his chosen land, put stakes up at each

The United States of America,

To all to whom these presents shall come, Greeting:

Homestead Certificate No. 1169.

Application 1597.

WHEREAS, There has been deposited in the GENERAL LAND OFFICE of the United States a Certificate of the Register of the Land Office at **Evanston, Wyoming,** whereby it appears that, pursuant to the Act of Congress approved 20th May, 1862, "To secure Homesteads to Actual Settlers on the Public Domain," and the acts supplemental thereto, the claim of

JOHN S. SHIVE

has been established and duly consummated, in conformity to law, for the south half of the southwest quarter and the southwest quarter of the southeast quarter of Section twenty-six and the northwest quarter of the northeast quarter of Section thirty-five in Township forty-five north of Range one hundred thirteen west of the Sixth Principal Meridian, Wyoming, containing one hundred sixty acres,

according to the Official Plat of the Survey of the said Land, returned to the GENERAL LAND OFFICE by the Surveyor General:

NOW KNOW YE, That there is, therefore, granted by the UNITED STATES unto the said **John S. Shive** the tract of Land above described; TO HAVE AND TO HOLD the said tract of Land, with the appurtenances thereof, unto the said **John S. Shive** and to **his** heirs and assigns forever; subject to any vested and accrued water rights for mining, agricultural, manufacturing, or other purposes, and rights to ditches and reservoirs used in connection with such water rights, as may be recognized and acknowledged by the local customs, laws, and decisions of courts, and also subject to the right of the proprietor of a vein or lode to extract and remove his ore therefrom, should the same be found to penetrate or intersect the premises hereby granted, as provided by law. And there is reserved from the lands hereby granted, a right of way thereon for ditches or canals constructed by the authority of the United States.

IN TESTIMONY WHEREOF, I, **Theodore Roosevelt** , President of the United States of America, have caused these letters to be made Patent, and the seal of the General Land Office to be hereunto affixed.

(SEAL)

GIVEN under my hand, at the City of Washington, the ....fifteenth........... day of ......October......, in the year of our Lord one thousand nine hundred and ....**eight**............, and of the Independence of the United States the one hundred and ....**thirty-third.**

By the President: _____

By _____, Secretary.

_____
Recorder of the General Land Office.

When homesteaders had "proved up," the U.S. Government sent them a patent to their land. The patent was signed by the President, and many homesteaders framed it and hung it on their cabin wall. Shive land patent, 1908. Bureau of Land Management.

corner, build a cabin, and start living in it. If he lived there for five years and improved the land as required—or "proved up," as it was called—he would get a deed from the government as soon as it had surveyed the land. This could take some time, and usually did. In Jack's case, his papers finally came through in 1908, in a document signed by President Theodore Roosevelt.

By that time, Jack's life had taken several more adventurous turns. In the summer of 1896, Lucy Nesbitt and her brother drove a herd of cattle into Jackson Hole from Montana. They traded and sold horses along the way and were also looking for pasture land where they could settle and raise horses. Here, Lucy met Jack Shive. As Lucy's daughter, Carrie, describes the meeting, "Jack had a one-room cabin, neat and shining as a new pin. When he met Mother he immediately began cutting logs to enlarge his home." They were married in the early spring of 1897, and Jack now had both a wife and a ten-year-old stepdaughter.

Jack Shive was always described as a man of few words. So it is fortunate for posterity that the family he married into had four generations of colorful women. All of them came to live on the ranch, and two of them—Lucy's daughter and granddaughter—published fine memoirs that give intimate glimpses of early homesteading in Jackson Hole and of the vivid personalities in the Shive family.

"When Gram married Gramp," writes Lucy's granddaughter, Frances, he was "a powerful, handsome Dutchman with a quick limp" who could outwork just about anybody and was already established on his ranch. "Gram was 39 years old. She was not beautiful—never had been; she wasn't even pretty . . . . Her coarsened skin and her white hair made her seem, upon first appearance, much older than Gramp (she was four years his senior), but not for long. Her high spirit, vitality, and rough gaiety could match those of anyone of any age." In Frances's portrait of her grandmother, Lucy bursts forth as a colorful, warm-hearted woman who did things that other women did not do, and who "didn't give a damn" what people thought. She could outride most men. She loved all flowers. And, though she had known sorrow and uncertainty before she came to Jackson Hole, she could still "laugh a mile" and often did.

Lucy grew up in the gold camp of Bannack, Montana. Like many children in the West at the time, she never went beyond the first few grades; and yet, like them, she read well, spelled well, and wrote what was then called a pleasing hand. This, too, was common in the West, and it speaks poignantly of homesteaders' efforts at self-education, and of their successes. In her teens, Lucy was inveigled into marriage by an old man. They had two children: a son who died in infancy, and a daughter, Fannie, who was a lifelong invalid. Lucy divorced the old man and hired herself out as a ranch hand, later as a chambermaid and waitress, and in time she ran her own boardinghouse.

Lucy's second husband was a good-looking young man who owned a photographic studio and who played in the town band. Unfortunately, he was also a drunkard. When their daughter, Carrie, was three and Fannie was thirteen, Lucy divorced him, "and took pride in hating him and whiskey the rest of her long life," writes her grand-daughter. She worked her way through hard years, always with the sorrow of Fannie's ill health. When Fannie died, Lucy "all but fought her heartache with her two fists. At last, being adventuresome, she made her way to the wild, remote Jackson Hole country. Here with John Shive she found her paradise. . . . Life began in this valley with her and Gramp, not beyond. The wind and the rain against her and the sun on her head—that was important. And work and laughter."

Shortly after their marriage, Lucy and Jack went to pick up Carrie, who had been staying with Lucy's parents on their Montana ranch. Written when she was an adult, Carrie's memoir of her trek from Montana to Wyoming and the beginning of her new life in Jackson Hole depicts a settler child's world. The difficulties of crossing the Tetons with seventy-five head of range cattle become real; and, through her observant and compassionate eyes, the character of quiet Jack Shive emerges.

Above: Lucy Shive prepares to go hunting about a year after she married Jack, c. 1898. Montana Historical Society, Helena.

Left: Lucy Shive's daughter, Carrie, on the Shive Ranch, c. 1913. Montana Historical Society, Helena.

"In mid-June Mother and Jack Shive came after me," Carrie wrote. "I looked Jack over, not critically, since I was ready and eager to like him, but very thoroughly, and he measured up. He was a tall, powerful man with a nice face, pale brown hair, and enormous hands. He was quick, quiet, and awkward as a boy. He seldom talked but when he did he had an abrupt, straightforward manner of speech which impressed one with his simple honesty. I have never known anyone who possessed such an amazing aptitude for attending to his own affairs, and he accorded to everyone else, even me, at the tender age of 10, the same privilege. He was Daddy Shive to me from the first hour I knew him and today, nearly forty years later, he is still my good father and friend."

Two cousins, George and Nig, accompanied Carrie, Lucy, and Jack on the trek from Montana. The total entourage included seventy-five cows and calves, five saddle horses, four pack horses, and five people. They followed wagon roads but took the cross-country trails where they could, camping at night by a spring or creek. It was slow, tiresome, and monotonous travel, and Carrie was only a child. "I hated the first week of that trip, burnt by the July sun and strangled by the dust. . . . At times Daddy Shive had to lift me from the saddle; I was too stiff, tired and sore to get down from Old Timberline without help. Even then the joints of my toes were sore."

On the eighth day they crossed the muddy torrent of the Fall River in Idaho. Carrie wrote,

> We crossed the northern end of the Teton Range by the Conant Trail route. For two whole days we wound up and over the mountains through pine woods, never seeing the lead cattle except when we rounded up for noon or night. The tenth day we camped in the upper end of Jackson Hole on the Snake River. That evening everyone in camp was apprehensive; the river was swollen by the fast-melting snow

in the high mountains until it was a wicked, vicious mael-
strom with driftwood dashing crazily down the current.

By daybreak, the river was a full foot higher. Not that it
mattered—we had to cross it, and we knew we had to swim.
A foot more or less in its depth made little difference. We
made short shrift of breakfast and breaking camp. The cattle
had not protested much at being driven into Fall River, but
it required all the powers of persuasion to get them into the
wild waters of Snake River. George cursed in English, Dutch
and several dialects. Nig yipped in his piercing countertenor
because singing to the cattle seemed ineffective in this case.
Daddy Shive bellowed and Mother yelled. I screamed and
the dog barked and bit, the black-snake whips popped and
yet the cattle milled and scattered between us and refused to
go into the water. . . . Finally, one old red cow grew weary of
the persistent abuse and dived in. The others immediately
followed. The calves bobbed like corks and the whole herd
drifted far down the river, swimming frantically.

Then it was Carrie's turn. "After they were across, Daddy Shive
took the bridle from my horse, Old Timberline, [and] then, tying a hal-
ter-rope around his neck, led him into the water. Daddy's horse, Gray
Eagle, was large and powerful, and swam high and strong. Timberline
was the tallest horse in our outfit and I, on my knees in the saddle, felt
the icy water reach up around my hips and I shivered and clung, scarce-
ly conscious of the cold." They were all soaked, but they got even the
tiniest calf across. "Then we realized we were half frozen in that cold
morning air, so we got off our horses and walked in our dripping
clothes." They still had the Buffalo River to cross the following afternoon, but after the Snake, even the cattle crossed this one obediently.
Then it was only two miles at a gallop to the ranch.

"I very definitely remember every detail of that first evening at home," wrote Carrie. Her mother was busy in the cabin, and the men were building beds for the cousins and setting up a tent for them. Carrie sat on a block of wood and watched the sun sink behind the Tetons. Even having to beat off swarms of mosquitoes with a willow switch did not stop her from being enthralled. In her memoir, she describes her experience:

"Gauzy pink clouds hung above the Teton Peaks. Long shafts of sunlight slanted through the deep canyons, then receded and at last were completely gone and the day seemed to pour out of the valley. A glorious afterglow flared for a few long minutes, then the last of the light drained through the canyons 'leaving the world to darkness and to me.'"

This lovely passage, ending with her poignant quote from Thomas Gray's 1750 poem, *Elegy in a Country Churchyard*, was written by a woman who hungered all her youth for a formal education and never got one. This kind of gift from early settlers like Carrie is a reminder to later generations to take nothing for granted about their lives.

Jackson Hole double-barreled skirt. The front panel of this skirt buttoned open to one side to create a divided skirt for ease of movement. In a "company" setting, the panel could be fastened across the front to conceal the divided skirt. Photo by Latham Jenkins / Circumerro Stock.com. Courtesy of Melinda Kornblum.

When Lucy and her daughter moved in, Jack Shive had not yet had time to complete his enlargement of their home, so it was still a one-room cabin. Here, Carrie gives an insider's view of an early settlers' home in Jackson Hole.

The cabin was comfortable and Mother had made it homey. A few photographs, framed, were hung on the walls, two gaily colored calendars gave the dates and a dash of color; a kind of plaque made from the wings and tail of a bluejay, artfully spread and tacked to the logs, intrigued me. I had never seen a jay and that particular shade of beautiful blue gave me a feeling of warmth and satisfaction I had never felt before in a color. The few pieces of furniture were home-made, solid, square and unlovely, but comfortable enough. . . . The one ornamental thing in the room was an antler chair Mother had made. Daddy Shive had quietly explained to me how she had ruined two saws, half a dozen bits, and a chisel working those antlers into the artistic piece of furniture. A red-and-white checked spread covered the table. A shining kerosene lamp stood exactly in the middle of it.

My bed was small and narrow and made especially for me. It had a marsh grass tick, with wild clover and mint scattered in with the grass, a wild goose feather mattress over that. Mother had sent to Sears and Roebuck, in Chicago, for sheets and pillow slips and an imitation candlewick coverlet. It was the sweetest smelling bed anyone ever slept in and few people today know the comfort and special dreams created by such a bed.

The first breakfast in the new home was pancakes, salt pork fried crisp, and scrambled eggs that had been thoroughly scrambled on the pack horse in the trek from Montana. The cousins asked what there was to do on the ranch. "Daddy answered dryly, 'Plenty. We have to finish the house. Sheds must be built for the cattle before winter comes. I have to make some corrals, and before the hay is ready to cut we have to get a mowing machine and a rake into the country. Got to go to St. Anthony for those things; it'll take a week for that trip. Then we have to put up the hay—should have a hundred tons, but we won't. We'll do the best we can, but the summer's short.' "

Carrie tells several stories about Jack Shive's special kindnesses to her. On that first morning, after she had finished washing the dishes,

Daddy Shive went to the corner of the room which was curtained off for a wardrobe and, prowling among his personal belongings, brought out a banjo. It was quite new and shiny and had ivory keys and a dashing red ribbon bow to hang it with. He handed it to me and told me in his serious, abrupt way that I could have it. I was speechless and awkward with pride and joy. Then he explained in a rather shy, apologetic way how he had gotten it. A young man whose name was Billy Miller came riding into the country. He had a saddle horse, and a pack mare, a bed, some food, a frying pan, and a banjo. The pack mare died giving birth to a colt, leaving him stranded. Now of all the things on the face of the earth, the most useless to Daddy Shive was a musical instrument. But Billy Miller had to have a pack horse, so Daddy traded him a very good one for the banjo, because it was the one article of Billy's impedimenta that he actually didn't have to have to continue his journeying about the country.

And a little later on that first day, another gift for Carrie. "Daddy Shive rode the hills around Sagebrush Flat and brought back his little bunch of horses. He had about ten head and among them was a mare named Topsy. She was small, black, and beautiful. When he got them

Carrie washing dishes in front of her mother's "wallpaper," n.d. Jackson Hole Historical Society and Museum, 1993.4825.060.

corralled he went in and tied a rope on Topsy and led her out to the bars where Mother and I were standing. He handed the rope to me, saying, 'She's yours. You can ride her. She's gentle—too gentle, you'll have to have spurs and a quirt to get anyplace. Go picket her out somewhere.' "

"I was delirious with the joy of my possessions," wrote Carrie. "A green world filled with flowers and trees, and trimmed with mountains; strange birds for friends, and for my very own a black mare. In my most extravagant flights of fancy I could never have thought of so much."

Life on the ranch was simple and uncomplicated, and full of work. Everyone pitched in. Haying went from daybreak to dusk. Lucy ran the mowing machine while Jack and the cousins raked, hauled, and stacked. Before getting onto the mower, Lucy planned and partially prepared their meals, and Carrie stayed around the cabin to cook and serve them. Even doing this heavy work, Lucy seldom wore trousers. According to her granddaughter, she usually wore a housedress or a shirtwaist with divided skirts made of khaki—known in Jackson Hole as double-barreled skirts—buttoned or hooked over a well-laced corset.

The ranch buildings, clustered at the far side of the west field, were entirely utilitarian. But when Jack built his first cabin he made sure that one window opened to the spectacular view of the Teton Range, and he later built Lucy a bay window. Elk were extremely numerous in Buffalo Valley, and the garden was enclosed by a fence made of elk horn that was "hilariously and laboriously gathered" by Lucy and Carrie. All the buildings had sod roofs. In the spring they were green with foxtail.

Inside, the newly enlarged cabin now included some of Lucy's things, brought in from Montana on a second trek. "There was the parlor organ," wrote Carrie, "some chairs, a rocker, a bureau, a barrel of dishes (they were china and had blue flowers on them, and I knew I would be very proud in Jackson Hole when we had neighbors in to dinner), a wood bedstead with springs and mattress."

Imagine hauling a parlor organ over the Teton Range. Now imagine the interior of the Shive log home, and Lucy decorating its walls. This is how Carrie's daughter, Frances, describes it: "Each spring the old house was papered inside with interesting material. Gram would make a trip down country with team and buggy, gathering magazines and newspapers. She was hardly home when they were slapped on the walls, which was always disappointing and frustrating to Mother, who was thirsty for knowledge; she always hoped for a little time to read before the magazines became a part of the house. But Gram could never see the necessity of learning through reading. However, she would condescend to hang the sheets right side up so that Mother could get a page of a story here, a column of an article there. And she gleaned, through opera glasses given her by a dude, what the ceiling had to offer."

Handmade rocker and table from Shive's homestead, known as the Hatchet Ranch. Photo by Latham Jenkins / CircumerroStock.com. Gift of Barbara Carlsberg. Jackson Hole Historical Society and Museum, 1996.0067.001 and 1996.0067.002.

Homesteaders rarely had fresh vegetables during the winter, and the Shive family was no exception. They had cabbage, and that was it. But they did get fresh meat: elk, antelope, even bear. Ranchers usually did not eat beef; their cattle were for selling and providing them an income. Jack was a skillful hunter. He was also a skillful cook, and he liked to prepare unusual treats like pickled bear's feet. Frances wrote, "We were very proud of Gramp's cooking. It never failed to be good. And the nearest he ever came to bragging was on his food. He said, 'If I have a frying pan and a little flour I kin live a long time in the mountains. But with you kids it's different. You've got to know something. You've got to git an education.' "

Lucy always had some winter handiwork in progress, and her embroidery was intricate and expertly done. "Now and again, of a winter evening, Gramp would pick up the embroidery and work ten or fifteen minutes, his huge hands dwarfing the piece," wrote Frances; "yet one could not tell where Gram left off and Gramp began—his work was that well done."

Jack and Lucy had now been married for a little over a year. Carrie had settled into her new and beloved home in Jackson Hole, and the crucial first wintering of the cattle was over. There was always more work to do on a ranch, especially in the summer. And yet, as the summer of 1898 moved into August with Jack busy harvesting hay, he took on what must have been the major adventure of his life: he joined the Owen-Spalding team and climbed the west face of the Grand Teton. By reaching the summit, he also became a key person in what may be the greatest American mountaineering controversy, still unresolved.

For sure, the team of William Owen, Franklin Spalding, Frank Petersen, and Jack Shive reached the 13,770 foot summit of the Grand Teton in 1898. But were they the first team to do so? After all, Nathaniel Langford and James Stevenson claimed that they had climbed the Grand Teton in 1872. In order to press his own claim that the Owen-Spalding team was the first to reach the summit of the

Above: The Owen-Spalding team in base camp preparing to climb the Grand Teton in August 1898. Left to right: Frank Petersen, Franklin Spalding, Thomas Cooper, Hugh McDerment, and Jack Shive. Photo by William Owen. Jackson Hole Historical Society and Museum, 1958.2700.001.

Left: Jack Shive, Franklin Spalding, and Frank Petersen pose for William Owen on top of the Grand Teton after their eleven-hour climb, 1898. Photo by William Owen. Jackson Hole Historical Society and Museum, 1958.2439.001.

Grand Teton, William Owen initiated a thirty-year struggle to disprove Langford and Stevenson's claim and to promote himself. None of his team companions ever worked for this recognition. Meanwhile, the full account of the Owen-Spalding climb was not told until *The American Alpine Journal* took up the story.

Published every year since 1929, *The American Alpine Journal* is the foremost annual record of significant mountaineering and rock-climbing ascents worldwide. In 1939, it published an article by Francis P. Farquhar finally giving the full account of the Owen-Spalding climb. While devastatingly polite about William Owen's grabbing of attention, Farquhar "brings into prominence the fine figure of Frank Spalding," as he put it. His account basically shows that Spalding was the leader of the climb, especially in the crucial final phase of reaching the summit, and that Jack Shive played a significant role in both the climb and in verifying Farquhar's account.

Spalding's own story appeared in the *Denver Evening Post* shortly after the climb. He also wrote letters to Nathaniel Langford, discussing the climb and comparing notes with him. These excerpts from the *Evening Post* give some of the key points in Spalding's description of the climb.

> The camp was right beneath the Grand Teton and it was a sight that I shall never forget, when early on the morning of the 11th we saw it wreathed with clouds and somber as if rebuking us for daring to scale it. We started at 5 o'clock . . . . Our outfit consisted of 450 ft. of rope, two ice axes, two iron-pointed prods, a half dozen steel drills, and twenty iron pegs. We made the top, however, without having to use the drills or pegs.
>
> The Matterhorn is climbed most easily by the north side. So was the Grand Teton. We decided to stick to the north, and cautiously made our way along our gallery until the man in front suddenly drew back with the remark that it ended in

a precipice that shot sheer down for 3000 ft. . . . The ledge was so narrow that we were forced to crawl on our stomachs. Even the consciousness that a fall would land us 3000 ft. below gave us a decidedly creepy sensation. We had to dig our fingers in the rough granite in places to pull ourselves along.

We followed a snow ridge for 200 ft. and then over the sharp, jagged eruptive rocks, so noticeable above the timber-line, clambered with a shout to the top. We made it at 4 o'clock exactly. We had been climbing for eleven hours.

Owen's photo of Shive, Spalding, and Petersen standing on the summit shows them wearing what appear to be ordinary leather boots and jeans, and ranchers Petersen and Shive seem to have on the hats they would have worn for haying. Two days later, Shive, Spalding, and Petersen returned to the summit to build a cairn and leave the team's names chiseled in the summit boulder.

A few hundred feet below the summit of the Grand Teton is the famous Enclosure, which both the Langford and Spalding teams indisputably did reach. "This remarkable feature," writes Farquhar, "has aroused the speculations of many subsequent visitors most of whom have undoubtedly had the same thoughts as Langford's, namely, that it was the work of Indians, that it was built for protection against the wind, and that it was constructed a long time ago." The indigenous people of the Jackson Hole area are known to have collected high-alpine plants in the Teton Range. And they had 11,000 years in which to explore all parts of the Range. The Enclosure gives rather a different perspective on who may first have climbed the Grand Teton.

Jack Shive did not care whether or not he was among the first to climb the Grand Teton, but he did care about the experience of the climb. It held so much meaning for him that he requested his ashes to be scattered on that great mountain after his death.

Jack Shive (right) in Buffalo Valley with Billy Owen, n. d. Both men participated in what is recognized as the first ascent of the Grand Teton. The climb was so meaningful to Jack that he requested his ashes be scattered over the mountain. Jackson Hole Historical Society and Museum, 1958.137.001.

Lucy's mother, Mary Jane Wadams, was a Montana woman who was famous for many things, including being the first white woman in Bannack, the boomtown that later became Montana's capital. Widely known as "Maw," she was also famous for being a cattle herder who carried an umbrella when she rode horseback. In Bannack's centennial in 1962, a young woman carrying an umbrella rode a horse up and down the street, representing Mary Jane Wadams.

After her husband died in 1902, Maw came to Jackson Hole to live with Lucy and her family. Maw officiated at the birth of her third great-grandchild, who was born on the ranch without a doctor and without mishap. This situation was common for homestead wives, though it was not always without problems. In her old age, Maw homesteaded 160 acres next to Jack and Lucy's land. She lived alone on her land in a one-room log cabin until she had proved up. Maw was in her eighties when she got her final papers in 1913.

Maw in her homestead cabin on the Shive Ranch, c. 1910. Jackson Hole Historical Society and Museum, 2005.0126.001.

Many women homesteaded. Most of them did so in the way Maw did, as part of a family that was expanding its holdings. Still, old as she was, she had to do her part. And she did. In *Second Life*, her great-granddaughter, Frances, writes of this late period in Mary Jane Wadams' life: "We shared the deep, slow summers of Maw's second life; the life she began by homesteading when she was an old woman. We were kids together, she in her early eighties, we three—Bill, Ruff, and I—not far from eight . . . Maw's land joined Gram and Gramp's, but her cabin was a mile from the buildings of the main ranch."

Jack Shive built Maw her one-room cabin. She did not have to live in it for the rest of her life, only for the three years then required for proving up. Her log cabin had a sod roof and a brushed earth floor that had been dampened and swept until it was as hard as cement. Unbleached muslin formed a low ceiling to make the room lighter and warmer in winter. "At sunup each morning Maw rose from the bed she had used more than one lifetime and built a fire," Frances wrote. "We children would be wakened by the scraping sound of the lifter moving over the stove as Maw, in her partial blindness, searched for the grooves that held the lifter. We three would watch her from the bed, our minds filled with the excitement of the coming day, our nostrils filled with the odor of burning pitch and sage."

On rainy days, a special treat for Frances and her brothers was the chance to smoke evergreen needles in corncob pipes. "We would first dry the needles in the oven and then grind them. Maw pretended we needed the pine smoke for a cough and head cold, and we pretended we had the cough and head cold so that we could sit around the little stove and smoke while she sang us crude songs in a high, dry voice, beating out time with a spoon against her teacup."

Frances and her brothers also got lessons in table manners from their great-grandmother. "Maw taught us to saucer and sip our tea as Thomas Jefferson had done over a hundred years earlier. And though her language was often crude, she taught us to say, 'I have a grand sufficiency,' when our little bellies were full."

Maw completed her homesteading duty and received her patent in 1913. She moved into a new cabin that was built for her near Lucy and Jack's home. Maw lived into her late eighties and was buried by her husband's side in Montana in 1921.

Jack and Lucy ranched very successfully for twenty-two years.

Opposite page: Maw Wadams, who was partially blind, began her day by firing up her wood cook stove and using the lifter to move the covers over the holes in the top of the stove. The sound of the lifter scraping the stove woke her grandchildren each morning. Photo by Latham Jenkins/CircumerroStock. com Courtesy of Ruth Hirsch.

This page: Maw's great granddaughter, Frances, with her horse, n.d. Jackson Hole Historical Society and Museum, 1958.3583.001.

Above: Jack and Lucy Shive on their ranch, n.d. Jackson Hole Historical Society and Museum, 1958.0195.001.

Right: Jack Shive at his woodpile in his later years, n.d. Jackson Hole Historical Society and Museum, 1958.0194.001.

Opposite page: The irrepressible Lucy Shive with two wolf cubs, n.d. Photo by Harrison Crandall. Jackson Hole Historical Society and Museum, Harrison Crandall Collection, 1991.4015.001.

They were good years, full of work and laughter. And dancing. The dancing was important. As a young man, Jack thought nothing of riding horseback or skiing forty miles to Jackson to dance after a full day's work. Lucy played the banjo or fiddle and called square dances at the same time. "Her playing was out of tune," writes her granddaughter, "but there was such zip to it no one could keep his feet still." In time, the dances moved north, and the Shives' ranch was the scene of many nightlong dances. As one guide to Jackson Hole describes it, "Teams of horses would jog in from miles around, loaded with gay people, food and children, and dance all night to the swingy calls of Grandma Shive."

When Jack and Lucy sold their ranch in 1919, it covered nearly eight hundred acres. They retired on a small place near Blackfoot, Idaho. This is where the man from the *American Alpine Journal* found Jack when he wanted to write his account of the 1898 climb of the Grand Teton. Lucy is buried with her daughter, Carrie, in the Blackfoot cemetery. Lucy "never tried to be anything but her own unbounded, funny self," as her granddaughter fondly remembered, and liked to pretend to swear at her grandchildren in Chinese. They never knew if she made up the Chinese words or had learned them as a child in the Montana mining camp. "Aflee-uumbaya-a . . . a-eunna-com-baya-a . . ." she'd swear at them, while Jack would watch and his face "would turn red with his silent laughter." When Jack died, his request was carried out. His ashes were scattered from an airplane over the mountain of his great adventure, the Grand Teton.

CHAPTER TWO

THE HANSEN FAMILY

ARRIVED IN JACKSON HOLE IN 1891

⊱┄◈┄○┄◈┄⊰

THE homestead era can seem far removed from us today. Most of the people who homesteaded were born more than a hundred years ago. Yet some of their lives leap from history, spanning in one lifetime the most amazing changes in culture and technology. A few of them, through hard work and good fortune, achieved the extraordinary in their lives. In their own individual way, they lived the American dream. Their stories are genuinely inspiring.

The story of Sylvia Irene Wood's life is such a story. She was born in 1885 in Rockland, Idaho, the sixth of eleven children. When she was seven years old, her family moved to Star Valley, Wyoming, where her father had acquired some land. They lived in an old log house that had only three rooms for their large family. "We kids slept three in a bed," Sylvia recalls in her account of her life. "In the summer the boys slept out in a shed." Her mother made a carpet for their home by sewing rags together, a common way for homestead women to create both warmth and beauty. Muslin covered the ceiling for its brightening effect and for warmth in the winter and was taken down once a year to be washed. Nothing was wasted.

In the fall, Sylvia's father and brothers traveled to Eagle Rock (now Idaho Falls, Idaho) to pick potatoes. This brought the family needed cash for buying winter supplies of food and clothing, she remembered. "Mother gave Father a list of yardages of cloth, buttons, thread, etc., needed for dresses for each of us, as well as shirts for the boys, and Father picked out all of the material. Then Mother made them up. His selections were very good, and one dress I got was made from a black material with a little rose bud in it, and I almost felt like a queen when wearing it." But one time his selection was not so good, and there was no exchange possible, since Eagle Rock was 50 miles away by horse and wagon. "He brought me home a pair of shoes with both shoes for the same foot. Needless to say, a trip back to town was out of the question, so there was nothing to do but wear them. I can remember standing in church or some other public place, trying to

Sylvia and Peter Hansen with their children, c. 1925. Clockwise from top center: Parthenia, Geraldine, Ordene, Robert, Helen, and Clifford. Courtesy of the Hansen family.

keep one foot hidden behind the other so people wouldn't notice."

Many homestead families lost one or more children at birth or early ages, mostly to disease. Many families lost their mother from birth-related illnesses. Both of these tragedies happened in Sylvia's family. Her three youngest siblings died in childhood. Her mother died after her eleventh pregnancy. "Mother was sick all the month of February. I cared for Elva, who was four, and always had charge of her. Mother lost another baby, a girl whose name was Isabelle. After that, Mother was very ill. One afternoon she called us children all to her bedside and told us good-bye. She kissed us and said, 'Sylvia, be a good girl.' I was nine years old."

Sylvia's father remarried less than a year after her mother's death. Even Sylvia, mild-spoken as she was, wrote that his new wife consistently favored her own son and was not very motherly toward his other children. He moved the family to the outskirts of Blackfoot, Idaho, where he rented an old ranch and kept twenty-one Holstein milking cows. Pound by pound, he and the boys hand-churned butter, which he took to Pocatello at four o'clock in the morning in a heavy lined box that held 50 pounds.

The younger children walked to a three-month country school. An older sister made their lunches: a meat sandwich and a syrup sandwich for each.

A few years later the family moved into the town of Blackfoot. Here Sylvia had to leave school for several years to take jobs keeping house and caring for children. Eventually, she made it back to grammar school, but she still had to work at jobs keeping house and caring for children. Good fortune entered Sylvia's life in the form of several supportive employers.

> Mrs. Osborn and Mrs. West (the Mayor's wife) encouraged me to go back to school. I had part of the fifth grade behind me. It wasn't easy, as I was larger than the rest of the

children. However, I made my grades, and Ben Holbrook gave me $2 a week for doing the washing, ironing, scrubbing, etc., after school. Most girls got $2.50 per week working all week without going to school. Mr. Holbrook's wife had died and left two small boys, whom I took care of and loved dearly. It nearly broke my heart to leave them when Mr. Holbrook married again and no longer needed me.

Then I went to work for Mrs. Osborn. The Osborns were my inspiration and mental builders. I kept house and canned the raspberries while Mrs. Osborn was away in California for six weeks. Mr. Osborn was like a father to me. I stayed with the Osborns and went to school, finishing the eighth grade. Mrs. Osborn was constantly pushing me, and when school finished, she had me take the teacher's examination. I was only able to get a third-grade certificate, and the Superintendent of Schools gave me a three-month school on Cedar Creek, which was about 16 miles above Blackfoot.

Sylvia boarded with Jake Baird and taught his ten-year-old son, Jake's three nephews, and a boy named Cliff. "That's where I got the name for my son. He was such a nice boy," she wrote. And here, she met Peter Hansen. "I received $45 per month, and when the three months were up, the two families said if I would teach for two more months, they would let me pick two yearling heifers from their cattle for my pay. This I did—except that Peter picked them out for me. He came often and was an old friend of the Bairds."

Peter Christofferson Hansen was born in Soda Springs, Idaho, on September 16, 1867. His parents had come with their parents from Denmark while they were in their teens. Like so many homesteaders, he came from a large family: six boys and three girls. His family took up a homestead 20 miles from Soda Springs, and Peter spent his childhood helping his father and brothers with their livestock business, learning the basic skills that would serve him so well in his adult life.

The family wintered their cattle on relatively warm bottomlands, where Peter spent four winters in a tipi caring for the cattle. In the winter of 1880–81, disaster struck. Two feet of snow fell during the early winter, and they ran out of hay. By spring, they had lost 200 head of cattle. "This taught me one valuable lesson," Peter notes in his autobiography, "that one must always have hay enough to feed whatever comes." He was thirteen years old, and he had learned the hard way the essential lesson of cattle ranching: wintering cattle meant feeding cattle through as many as six or seven months, and that could mean harvesting as much as several hundred tons of hay every summer. The question, "How did you winter?" was a question of survival.

Peter attended school whenever he could, fitting in his education with cattle ranching and jobs where he could find them. He cut the logs for a schoolhouse that later became the family's home for several years. He got a job with a large cattle outfit and barely survived a night's cattle stampede. In Deer Lodge, Montana, staying with his father's parents, he attended the local college. He worked in Oregon building brick houses. It rained all the time, so he headed for California and worked in the lumber business before returning home and spending three years at the Utah Agricultural College.

He was twenty-nine years old when he first saw Jackson Hole and was so impressed that he decided to settle in the valley. He filed a homestead claim on 160 acres in Wilson, just south of what is now Teton Village, and spent the next winters in his Idaho home while proving up his homestead every summer. When he met Sylvia Wood, he found love. He was thirty-eight years old and she was twenty when they were married at the home of her beloved Osborn family. Together, Peter and Sylvia would build an enduring love, a caring and prosperous family, and a beautiful ranch that survives to this day. One of their sons would become Governor of Wyoming and later a U.S. Senator. It was the beginning of the American dream.

The start was tough. Although Peter owned a house and land in Idaho and had a good credit rating at the bank, he and Sylvia started from scratch in Wyoming. Their homestead had a one-room log cabin with a stove and two chairs. They had to make the bed and everything else. Every day they went into the field to clear the land. This meant grubbing sagebrush, the bane of Jackson Hole homesteaders. Here is their son Cliff's description of the process:

> One of the first jobs that the early ranchers had was to try to grow some grass so they could keep their livestock over the winter. Because sagebrush was everywhere, the job was to get rid of the sage. Now that could be accomplished in different ways. One way was to take a grubbing hoe, or an ax, and chop it off at its roots. Another way was to irrigate. Sage is not very tolerant of irrigation. A third way was to burn it, and sometimes that was an effective way, but you had to control the fire. Anyway, Dad also devised another way to get rid of it. That was to take a big heavy log, perhaps eight or ten feet long, and attach to it a piece of railroad rail. And there were four horses hitched onto that rail. It would uplift the sagebrush in great style, tear it out, and go back over the log. And then they could ignite those sagebrush piles, and that was their way of getting rid of it.

Every day that first summer, Peter and Sylvia grubbed and piled and burned and plowed and irrigated. At harvest, their field provided five tons of hay.

After harvest, they took jobs on the building of Jackson Lake Dam at Moran. Through fall and into winter, they lived in tents on the dam site. Peter hauled freight with two teams of horses; Sylvia cooked for eight men. "For Christmas dinner, I made pudding and candy, and that was all the Christmas we had," she wrote. "The next day we left for home, as the coffer dam was finished. About a foot of snow had fallen that night, and I had to use a hammer to pound the wheels as we went along, to break loose the heavy snow that piled up between the spokes. We pitched our tent on Cottonwood Creek that night. Peter shoveled the snow away, set up our stove, and we were comfortable. The next day we made it home."

For two years they spent their winters in Idaho, bringing cattle across Teton Pass to their Wilson homestead in the summer and selling the cattle before returning to Idaho. This was how Peter first became known in Jackson Hole as a cattle dealer. Eventually, they bought a ranch in Zenith, a settlement that was about a mile west of the present Jackson Hole Golf & Tennis Club, and lived there until 1916. By this time, they had four children: Parthenia, age nine, Geraldine, age seven, Clifford, age four, and Helen, age two. They also still had the homestead in Wilson, and this meant that Peter had to irrigate land on both sides of the Snake River. There was no bridge, so he had to ford the river on horseback twice a day, every day. As Cliff Hansen remarked in

Construction of the concrete Jackson Lake Dam as it looked in 1915, a year before it was completed. Like Peter and Sylvia Hansen, many locals worked on this enormous project. Photo by Floyd Bous. Jackson Hole Historical Society and Museum, 1958.0769.001.

a recent speech, "I dare say I know of no one who has forded the Snake River as many times as my Father did."

Most Jackson Hole homesteaders worked at occasional jobs to augment their income, and Peter was no exception. There was the Jackson Lake Dam job, and then his contract to carry the mail from Jackson to Zenith for $23.83 a month, which meant fording the Gros Ventre River and trying to keep snowy roads open. Sylvia kept house and raised children, and she took on the job of making and selling butter, which paid for needed ranch equipment. Their daughter Parthenia recalls, "Those were hard years. We never had so much as one nickel to spend, not ever! I remember one kid at school would always have a dollar to spend, and we thought that was something. That dear girl used to treat us all once in awhile."

Having no extra money did not mean having no fun. "We just made our own fun. My Mother was a person that loved to entertain and have people. She'd do the best she could and entertain neighbors. She could always think of games for the whole group to play. It didn't make any difference what age anybody was, they'd all play the games."

Everyone worked, the younger children too. "We all worked as soon as we were able to do anything," said Parthenia. When he was seventy-seven, Cliff still remembered taking cattle to the summer range when he was a boy. It was a ten-day trip. Sylvia took care of the children, drove the team, and cooked. The two older girls were already good riders and worked as ranch hands. Little Cliff helped Sylvia. "Mother was the most important part of the crew. She loaded the chuck wagon, she loaded the beds, she pitched the tents if that was necessary, and she cooked the meals and wrangled a few kids as well. I remember making that trip, and it was a great trip."

Taking a herd of cattle to market involved herding it over Teton Pass to Victor, Idaho. In those days, the dirt road went straight up one side of the pass and straight down the other, with no switchbacks. As Parthenia describes it, there were usually five riders herding about two

Top: Sylvia Hansen and her son Cliff on their way to the summer cattle range, c. 1916. "This looks like a picnic," said Cliff Hansen when he was in his nineties, "but it was actually hard work for everyone." Jackson Hole Historical Society and Museum, Parthenia Stinnett Collection, BC.0103. Bottom: Winter feeding on the Hansen Ranch. This essential feeding of cattle could go on for as long as six or seven months, n.d. Jackson Hole Historical Society and Museum, BC.0284.

to three hundred cattle. "When we herded the cattle, we gathered the ones that we were going to ship right in our west field. We had early lunch, gathered those up and drove them through the draw and came out at the Jimmy Brown ranch. Then we took them over to the old Davis place on the hill. Then, the next trip, we would go up on the hill and herd them over to Victor. It would take about a day and a half. That accounts for my many times over the Pass on horseback." They got about five to six cents per pound for their cattle.

All of the family's efforts went toward buying land and raising cattle. In 1918, the Hansens bought the Redmond Ranch and cattle, and next summer the family moved to Spring Gulch, where the Hansen Double T Ranch still is. Life was getting a bit easier. They were much closer to the town of Jackson, whose amenities included electric power, a school, a doctor, a new hospital, a dentist, a bank, a telephone exchange, a drugstore, the Elk Cigar Store, a billiard parlor, two hotels, and two general mercantile stores.

Still, it was a long way from the Hansen home to the school, and

The Spring Gulch school bus, typical of school buses in Jackson Hole in the 1920s. Jackson Hole Historical Society and Museum, Parthenia Stinnett Collection, BC.0096.

the county did not plow any roads in those days. So they bought a house in town, and Sylvia moved into it with the children in winter, so the older girls could go to school. After living alone one winter, Peter said to Sylvia, "If I build a school sleigh, will you stay home?" She agreed, and Peter built Jackson Hole's first school sleigh. It was canvas covered, with a wood-burning stove bolted to the floor and a bench along each side. For four years, it transported the Hansen children and neighboring Charter children to school. The trip took about one hour each way.

One of the lovely and touching things about Sylvia Hansen was her capacity for creating joy in her life, like the way she organized parties and games, even when there was no money. And the way she learned to paint: "Mrs. Horton taught school and art, and the days she had art I took Cliff and went to school. He would sit on the seat by me (never any trouble) while I learned to paint. How I loved it! And painted three pictures by myself."

Neighbors helped neighbors when Jackson Hole was being settled. When Sylvia came down with pneumonia in the fall of 1921 and was in the hospital for nine days, her neighbor Mrs. Charter took in all four Hansen children. There were two more Hansen children to come: Ordeen in July, 1922, and Robert in July, 1924.

Cliff Hansen stuttered terribly as a child. When he first started school, his teacher sent him home and told his mother that he was relatively "uneducable." Fortunately, his mother had been a teacher. He stayed out of school for a year. Since speaking was so difficult for him, Sylvia concentrated on math with him, and he became one of the better math students in his class. To this day, her son expresses his gratitude for her dedicated concern and patience. Cliff continued stuttering until he was almost fifteen years old, when his parents sent him to the Benjamin N. Bogue Institute in Indianapolis. The six weeks he spent at the clinic changed his life. In a 1993 interview he muses, "You wonder what motivates one. I must say that the men on the ranch were,

Top: Peter C. Hansen, rancher and public servant, on his horse, 1930s. Jackson Hole Historical Society and Museum, 1958. 0020.001.

Right: Cliff Hansen as Governor of Wyoming, 1962–1967. Jackson Hole Historical Society and Museum, 1958.1130.001.

Opposite page: Cliff and Martha Hansen have fun posing for the *Planet Jackson Hole* newspaper outside their home on the Hansen ranch, December 2004. Photo by Cameron Neilson. Courtesy *Planet Jackson Hole*.

overall, a very kindly bunch. But I remember one day one of the fellows saying, 'Well, don't you worry, Cliff, someday you'll be Governor.' And I thought, 'I'll show you birds, I'll be Governor.' " And so he was, from 1962 to 1967, before he became a United States Senator. Historian T. A. Larson writes that "his unaffected manner, modesty, willingness to learn, and engaging personality caught the fancy of Democrats as well as Republicans."

Busy as their lives were, Peter and Sylvia still took an active part in community affairs. Sylvia served on the high school board for nine years and as vice president on the hospital board for thirteen years; she was president of the local Red Cross, the P.T.A., and the hospital guild for one year each. Peter was one of Teton County's first commissioners and served for eleven years. He was elected state senator in 1937 and spent two years in the state capital, Cheyenne. He also served as president and honorary member of the Jackson Hole Cattle and Horse Association, and on the executive board of the Wyoming Stock Growers Association. Late in life, he was vice president and director of the Jackson State Bank.

He was also still a rancher who owned several ranches, and he remained an active rancher into old age. When he sold his Green River Ranch, he took some help and trailed the Hansen purebred herd of some two hundred and fifty head to the Charter range on the headwaters of the Gros Ventre River. This was a long trip, and it meant crossing the Continental Divide. "I have often thought," says his son Cliff, "what a physical effort that was for a man of his age, over 80 years. Needless to say, they camped out along the way."

Meanwhile, Sylvia had decided to take flying lessons. She was fifty-nine years old. "One morning I flew over the school house at recess time, and the teacher told me later they heard and saw the plane, and young Peter said, 'Oh, that's just my grandmother.' "

In their older years, Peter and Sylvia's life together was finally getting easier. Their lifelong hard work now allowed them pleasures they had neither the time nor the money for in their earlier years. They began to travel—easy pleasures like sailing on the famous *Lurline* to Hawaii, and hardy adventures like riding horseback at night to see the red flow of lava from Mexico's great Uruapan Volcano.

But Peter was eighty-five years old and finally getting frail. In the fall of 1952, he became ill. He was taken to the Jackson hospital, where he died. Sadly, Sylvia was in a Denver hospital for an operation and could not be with him at the end. "He left us November 26, 1952. A wonderful husband and father," Sylvia said in her autobiography.

"My Mother stayed on the ranch until December, 1961," says Parthenia. "She had built a house in town, and she moved into town then. While she was still on the ranch, she decided to see some more of the world." And see the world she did, from Europe to South America to the Orient. She returned to Jackson in time to move into her new house before Christmas. She was seventy-six years old.

Town was the perfect place for Sylvia for the rest of her life. "My mother was the hardest worker and the most efficient worker I have

Sylvia Hansen—a long and wonderful life, n.d. Courtesy *Jackson Hole News and Guide*.

ever been around in my life," says Parthenia. "When she moved into town she had a wonderful time entertaining. She was right in the center of things, and she loved her friends and all the activities. And, I must say, she deserved it!"

Sylvia Hansen was ninety years old when she died in Jackson at St. John's Hospital on January 24, 1976. She had lived a rich life. "Jackson Hole lost one of its best-loved pioneers," announced the *Jackson Hole News*. "She was always helping people," said an earlier article in the *Jackson Hole Guide*. "There always was somebody who needed taking care of, and she was a real neighbor. Probably nobody knows how much she's done . . . The beautiful ranch they created with hard labor and a deep love of the land stands out today as a successful landmark in our valley."

Sylvia herself made these comments about her life: "I guess perhaps the proudest moment of my life was in January of 1963, when Cliff was inaugurated as Governor of Wyoming. All of our family was there except Robert, who was then living in California." This was indeed a long way to have come for the motherless girl who had to work her way through grammar school. "What a wonderful life I have had. From covered wagons to landing men on the moon. Such a life span! I thank the Lord for all I have been able to see and do, for He has been very good to me." Peter and Sylvia Hansen are buried in a simple grave in the Aspen Hill Cemetery in Jackson.

CHAPTER THREE

THE FERRIN FAMILY

ARRIVED IN JACKSON HOLE IN 1898

>·+·+>·-0·-<+·+·<

I F Jackson Hole ever had a cattle baron in the Western tradition, Josiah David Ferrin would fit the role. He was called "Uncle Si" by many local people and, was also known as the "Cattle King of Wyoming." These nicknames fit the character of Si Ferrin, who was big and rugged and sometimes talked dialogue right out of a movie western, and who was also a devoted father to fourteen children.

Si was born in Eden Valley, Utah, in 1873. According to his son Merritt, he first came to Jackson Hole in 1898. He was the trail boss for a cattle buyer who bought all the cattle in the valley that were for sale, and then drove the herd to Idaho. When Si saw the Buffalo Bench in the Buffalo Fork area of Jackson Hole, he said, "I'm going back to Utah and get my family and come back." This was a man who loved the Tetons from the first moment he saw them, and who was to say near the end of his life, "I've been looking at them for 46 years, but I've never known a moment when the Tetons didn't stir my soul."

Back in the Eden Valley, Si was so eloquent that fifteen families traveled with him when he left two years later for Jackson Hole. That year was very wet. The ground was so soft that the travelers often had to fasten big cottonwood logs under the wagons. The logs became skids when the wheels sank in too far, and the horse teams had to be doubled up to pull the wagons through the mud. It was tough going— tough enough to make some travelers reconsider. And some did. When they finally reached St. Anthony, Idaho, on the west side of the Tetons, ten of the fifteen families decided this was far enough. "They didn't have the same stamina as the people who left Missouri and started for Oregon," said Merritt Ferrin. Si, with his wife and their three sons, two of his brothers, his wife's brother, and one friend went on across the mountains with their families to Jackson Hole.

Here, a major disappointment awaited them: homesteading in the Buffalo Bench area had been closed by the Forest Service. A movement

Si Ferrin was credited with many firsts in Jackson Hole. This photo of him in 1942 is from the article, "Gentleman Who Brought First Elk Out of Hole Still Sturdy." Jackson Hole Historical Society and Museum, Vertical Files.

to have the United States Congress reverse this decision had not yet succeeded. Until it did succeed, Si had to make do with filing a desert claim on land in the Flat Creek area. The story goes that he loaded a plow on his wagon and went out to start proving up on his land. Soon he came home, saying, "Hell, I hooked the team on the plow and tried to make a furrow. It was so rocky I couldn't even get the plow into the ground. I just looked around and couldn't see a place that wasn't rocky, so I loaded the plow up and came home." He sold the property and moved on.

Next, he took up a claim on Twin Creek in what is now the National Elk Refuge, where he successfully raised oats, wheat, and barley. In 1902, he reportedly was the first in Jackson Hole to harvest oats as grain, a practice later taken up by many ranchers in the valley to insure a harvest in a growing season that was often cut short by snow. When Si saw that his oat crop was going to ripen, he began to look around for ways to harvest it. In Victor, Idaho, he met a man who had a threshing machine. As Merritt Ferrin tells it, "My father told Mr. Bailey that he had 40 acres of grain over in Jackson Hole, and if he could talk him into bringing his thresher over, he would buy a binder from him. Mr. Bailey said that he was already on his way over the Pass with the thresher. I can still remember that threshing machine. They used horsepower—10 head of horses—and threshed the grain." The binder he bought was the first in the valley and one of Si Ferrin's many firsts. As he reminisced to a newspaper many years later, "People from all over the Hole used to come to see [how] that contraption operated."

Another story, this one about Si and the sawmill, illustrates two realities of early homestead life in Jackson Hole: The neighborly help that was readily available, and the difficulties of getting over Teton Pass in winter. According to Merritt Ferrin, the story went like this: The Johnson brothers wanted to bring a sawmill and boiler over the Pass from Rexburg, Idaho, and it was winter. Si and his brother-in-law went over to help them. "They had quite a wrestle. The sleighs wouldn't carry the boiler when they got to the deep snow on the hill. They didn't have big enough sleighs, so they had to make a sleigh. When they got to the steep part of the mountain, they had to go straight up the canyon hill. Of course, they used block and tackle on their wagons. When they got to the top, they had an awful time getting that boiler down the hill. You couldn't put on a cross log because of the rocks and stumps, so they finally wrapped chains around the runners of the home-made sleigh, cut a couple of big red fir trees to pull behind it, and eventually got down." They set up the sawmill in the mouth of Curtis Canyon, which adjoins today's National Elk Refuge.

In 1901, while he still lived in the southern part of the valley near what would become the town of Jackson, Si helped to lay out the town site. He reportedly also opened the first saloon in Jackson Hole. Already, he was establishing himself as a man of powerful energy and a jack of many trades, who sought opportunities wherever they beckoned and who initiated quite a few opportunities on his own.

Tragedy struck Si and his family when his wife, Emmeline, died after giving birth to their fifth son. Si was left alone with four young sons and a baby. As usual, people helped out. Si's sister, who had three little girls of her own, took in his five motherless sons. This connection with his sister's family was how Si came to know Edith McInelly, who would become his second wife.

In her handwritten sketch of her life, Edith McInelly Ferrin tells of being born on January 26, 1885, in London, England, the daughter of George and Elizabeth Goldthorpe. They separated shortly after her birth. Her mother found employment in a hospital and placed Edith in a day nursery. A year later her mother's Uncle Tom, who had emigrated to Utah, was in England on a mission for the Mormon Church. He talked with her mother about the Church and the opportunities in America and was so encouraging that her mother decided to join him as soon as possible. The next year he sent passage funds for baby Edith and her mother to come to Utah. They were ten days aboard ship and

Portrait of Josiah D. Ferrin, age twenty, given to his wife Emmeline at the time of their wedding, 1893. Jackson Hole Historical Society and Museum, Gift of the Ferrin Family, 2005.0153.005.

ten more on a train, and then they were met by Uncle Tom with his wagon and team of horses and went on to their new home, camping on the way. Thanks to Uncle Tom's generosity, they had what for that time was a relatively easy and comfortable journey to the West.

Edith's mother married Gilbert McInelly a few years after their arrival in Utah. He was doing well in Utah, but he got the "wandering bug," according to Edith, and took his family with him. After several moves, they settled in Victor, Idaho, where their neighbors from Utah now lived. Edith was twelve years old and had very little education. She went to work for a couple from whose ranch she could walk to a summer school. When she was fifteen, she was working for John Bailey and his family, and came with them when they settled in Jackson Hole. This was Mr. Bailey of the Si Ferrin grain thresher and binder story. Edith worked for various valley families and then went on to help Si

Edith Ferrin with Merritt and Emily, two of the fourteen children she and Si raised, c. 1909. Courtesy *Jackson Hole News and Guide*.

Edith, Emily, and Ada Ferrin—three of Si and Edith Ferrin's daughters, 1914. Jackson Hole Historical Society and Museum, Gift of the Ferrin Family, 2005.0153.004.

Top: Clay Seaton, Bob Crisp, and Ray Ferrin on the mail stage in early Jackson, 1924. Jackson Hole Historical Society and Museum, 1958.516.001. Bottom: Bob Ferrin riding a bucking bronc at the famous Elbo Rodeo beneath the Grand Teton, c. 1925. Photo by S. N. Leek (BC.0405). S. N. Leek Collection, American Heritage Center, University of Wyoming.

Top: Two of Si Ferrin's sons, half brothers Merritt and Glen posing for the camera on a hunting trip with friends and clients, 1932. They are pictured 3rd and 5th from the left, respectively. Jackson Hole Historical Society and Museum, 1993.4933.015. Bottom: Ben Goe, Ed Lumbeck, and Glen Ferrin showing off their catch, n.d. Photo by Boots Allen. Jackson Hole Historical Society and Museum, 1958.1273.001.

Ferrin's sister with housework and the care of her three little girls and Si's five sons.

Two years later, Edith married Si Ferrin. She had just turned twenty, and he was thirty-two. It is no mean task to marry a man who has five sons, the oldest only ten years younger than you are. She must have been a young woman of strength and fortitude, and with a big heart. In her life sketch she writes, "Undoubtedly this marriage was brought about through my taking care of Si's boys and the love their father bestowed upon them and the love we all shared together." Si and Edith eventually had nine children, four sons and five daughters. With Si's five boys, that made nine sons and five daughters in the Ferrin family.

In the spring of 1907, the land Si longed for on the Buffalo Bench was finally released for settlement by the Forest Service. Si had sent his congressman a letter asking that he be notified the minute the land was open. He had waited for seven years, and he was ready. How he managed to secure his land is another Si Ferrin story told by old-timers.

This is how his son Merritt remembers it: Si and his friend Ralph were working for the Wyoming Game and Fish Department and were camped on the shores of String Lake when a boy arrived at the camp with two special delivery letters, one for each of them. This was the long-awaited notification. Each man scanned his letter and said nothing. There were only three or four parcels of land left on the Buffalo Bench, and they both knew that they wanted the same parcel. It was a fine site near the mouth of the Buffalo River, with a spring and an abandoned cabin. "The next morning they started to pack up and Ralph said to Dad, 'Which way are you going? Are you going by the Ferry or by Moran?' At that time of year the Snake River was running high. Dad said he wasn't going by either one, he was going straight through. Ralph said, 'And swim the river?' Dad told him, 'Why, yeah.' Ralph then said he was going by Moran and he hoped Dad drowned. When Ralph finally got to the land, Dad had his corners staked out and was getting himself something to eat. Ralph rode up and said, 'Well, you didn't get drowned, so let's go over and stake my place.' " Local lore has it that Si offered Ralph some of his supper before they went.

Si got his land, and next year he and Edith settled on the Buffalo property with their children. They cleared 50 acres, raised timothy for hay, and built a house, corrals, barns, and other outbuildings. Si valued this proving up at $5,000. In addition to being a farmer and rancher, Si also hauled freight, cut and hauled timber, and operated a sawmill. He secured a lucrative contract to supply beef to the Reclamation Service when it was building the Jackson Lake Dam. He also secured the Jackson-to-Moran mail run, earning $3,000 per year for service three times per week. It was a reliable source of income, but the work could be dangerous. Two mail carriers had already died in avalanches and one drowned while fording the Gros Ventre River.

These were good years for the family. Between 1911 and 1928, Si

This kerosene-fired tractor was Jackson Hole's first. Not surprisingly, it belonged to Si Ferrin and was in use in 1917 on his Elk Ranch. Jackson Hole Historical Society and Museum, 1958.1288.001.

purchased six other spreads, including the Elk Ranch, in the vicinity of his place on the Buffalo Bench. As their sons came of age, they also took up homesteads, and in 1913 Edith got her own homestead patent—all adding further to the ranch and the Ferrin Land and Cattle Company.

Si Ferrin stories continued to be told across the valley. He was a colorful character, and one who was held in affectionate esteem. The Si Ferrin stories highlighted situations that were familiar to people in Jackson Hole, and gave them a humorous twist. Here is one about Si's battle to keep hungry elk from gobbling up his winter haystacks, a standard problem for Jackson Hole ranchers and homesteaders. High fences and dogs failed to stop the elk. Then Si erected a scarecrow and hung a lantern on it to keep the elk away at night. "How did it work?" someone asked him. "Didn't," he replied. "Next morning an elk came down to the house to get more oil for the lantern."

Si Ferrin as one of Wyoming's most famous game wardens. Stories about his colorful and effective ways of handling poachers and tusk hunters were very popular in Jackson Hole, n.d. Jackson Hole Historical Society and Museum, 1958.2187.001.

Si became a leader in community projects, sports, and politics. But it was his activities as a deputy game warden that won him statewide fame. He was a game warden for fourteen years and was hailed for his work in apprehending poachers and tusk hunters, men who killed elk for their eye teeth or tusks. In his book *Early Jackson Hole*, old-timer Marion Allen tells this story about Si and a gang of poachers who would kill an elk just to get its teeth.

"There was one character in Jackson who was a member of the Purdy and Binkley gang of poachers," wrote Allen.

> He was sometimes called "Dutch." The most popular item with them was elk teeth—for they were small and portable and had a ready market. A pair of bull elk teeth would bring $10 and up. This was at a time when $30 a month was considered good wages—if there was a job to be had. Well, Dutch was quite a "loud mouth" and was always walking around Si, rattling something and making remarks about the elk teeth he had. Si ignored this for several days, but as Dutch became more and more brazen and was bragging that Si was afraid of him, it began to get on Si's nerves. Si was a powerfully built man and was easy to get along with but at last, without any warning, he grabbed Dutch, pinned him down, pulled out a pocket knife and proceeded to cut off Dutch's pockets. When they were emptied, they were found to contain nothing but a handful of gravel—no elk teeth. This put an abrupt end to Dutch or anyone else razzing Si for a long, long time.

The last trip Merritt Ferrin remembers his Dad making as a game warden was in about 1920, when Si went up to Two Ocean Pass and brought back a hunting party who had killed several moose, which was illegal. "They admitted that they were at fault, but said they had no horses in camp. They sent their horse wrangler out, and he came back and said he couldn't find the horses. They said they couldn't go without the horses. Dad said, 'Well looks like you are all pretty well shod. You had better take on a pretty good feed, because it's a long ways to walk to the Shives' Ranch.' That was the closest they could get anything to eat. Dad said, 'I'll give your horse wrangler about 30 minutes more to find some horses, then we're heading down the trail.' The wrangler found the horses all right." The poachers were later fined $500.

The Elk Ranch continued to prosper. In peak years the Ferrins ran about two thousand head of cattle on their four thousand acres and harvested about six thousand tons of hay. "When it came time to put up the hay, it took a 25-man crew and 50 head of horses some 25 working days to get the job done. Feeding the crew was an around-the-clock job," according to Edith. "It took a beef a week and 50 pounds of flour every other day just to keep them going." Those were good times. "You couldn't get that group of people or a group of people like that togeth-

Haying at the Elk Ranch during the peak years when it took twenty-five men and fifty horses to do the job, n.d. Jackson Hole Historical Society and Museum, Gift of Triangle X Ranch, BC.0231.

er again," Merritt fondly remembers. "We'd have a dance after the beef were gathered just before they were shipped, about the middle of September. We'd clean the hay out of the big barn and dance upstairs." There were trips outside the valley with the steers in the fall, rodeos at the Elbo Ranch, automobiles, and a big house in town. The Elk Ranch was the largest outfit in Jackson Hole, and Si Ferrin had become the largest taxpayer in the county.

And then times changed drastically for the worse for Jackson Hole ranchers, and for Si. The agricultural depression of the 1920s was a heavy blow to Wyoming. Depressed cattle prices hit ranchers and Jackson Hole's economy hard, and gloom characterized the mood of the people in the valley. For Si, things got so bad that he mortgaged his property for $205,362 to keep his operation going. According to county records, he managed to pay off most of the loan. Still, his attempt to save his ranch failed, and eventually he went broke.

He was not alone. As early as 1920, veteran Jackson Hole ranch-

er Bill Crawford had lunch with Yellowstone National Park superintendent Horace Albright about the plight of Jackson Hole ranchers. He told Albright that "people were destroying the lives of themselves and their families by trying to ranch in this country" and that unless their ranches were bought out, he and all the other ranchers would oppose Albright's proposed extension of Yellowstone National Park to include part of Jackson Hole. Crawford hoped that the government or private parties could finance such a scheme. In 1921, Si Ferrin and Bill Kelly discussed a similar plan with Albright. Horace Albright's papers from the early 1920s contain numerous letters about the economic troubles of ranchers in Jackson Hole. In late 1923, he was able to testify that "practically every ranchman in Jackson Hole is broke and in debt up to his ears. There is no hope of these poor people getting out of debt."

The ranchers were not the only ones who could see the future threatening their livelihood. Dude ranchers were beginning to reach the same conclusion, but for a different reason. For them, the threat was the increasing tourism and the commercialization of the most beautiful parts of Jackson Hole. Both cattle ranchers and dude ranchers saw a serious threat to their livelihood, and both also felt a genuine concern that their magnificent valley would be mutilated. Petitions to preserve the valley began to appear. Si Ferrin was involved with the first one in 1923, and in later ones.

Hard times seem to have hit a peak in 1925, and the petitions became more specific about solutions. In that year, ranchers circulated a petition supporting a buyout of private lands. Si Ferrin and Pierce Cunningham are said to have composed most of the petition, and to have circulated it for signatures. "We have tried ranching, stock raising," said the petitioners, "and from our experience have become of the firm belief that this region will find its highest use as a playground. That in this way it will become the greatest wealth-producing region of the State." These were prophetic words, and the years since 1925 have certainly proved them to be accurate. "The destiny of Jackson's Hole is as a playground, typical of the West, for the education and enjoyment of the Nation, as a whole," said the petitioners, and pledged to sell their ranches at what they considered a fair price. Remarkably, ninety-seven landowners endorsed the petition, many of them Jackson Hole's first settlers and former opponents of this idea.

It was John D. Rockefeller, Jr., who eventually would save the destitute ranchers and the valley. His great gift to the people of the United States would not come to fruition for many years and will be explored in a later chapter of this book. But already in the 1920s, Rockefeller's Snake River Land Company was carrying out the petitioners' two main ideas: It was buying private lands from willing sellers, and it was holding those lands until an agency could be found to administer them for the public good.

Yet another blow hit Si Ferrin in 1929, when the Forest Service cut the cattle-grazing permits that were essential to ranchers in Jackson Hole, and also advised him that in a few years the permits would be decreased again. That did it. Si decided it was time to sell the Elk Ranch. "I fought like the very devil to keep him from selling," Edith Ferrin said, "but he was determined, so we sold out and moved to town."

The Ferrins sold their holdings to the Snake River Land Company in 1928–29. The company paid them $114,662.12 for their 3,629 acres and improvements, a fair price at the time. In the autumn of 1929, Si took his last big herd of cattle over the mountains to Sugar City, Idaho. He was beaten as a rancher, but he was still Si Ferrin. When asked how many cattle were in his herd, he quipped in true character, "Dunno—ain't none of us can count, but there must be 30–40 acres of 'em!"

He divided the money from the Snake River Land Company among his family and invested his money in cattle, starting a feedlot operation in Sugar City run by his son Merritt. Meanwhile, back in Jackson Hole, he continued to support the plan to preserve the valley by creating a national park.

Then the Great Depression hit him. The Wall Street stock-market crash of 1929 precipitated the worst economic downturn in the history of the United States and had devastating effects across the country. The depression lasted for over a decade, with hundreds of thousands of Americans losing their jobs, financial institutions collapsing, and businesses failing.

The depression left Si irrevocably bankrupt. He never really recovered from this final blow. In his last years, he worked for his brother-in-law as a night watchman and as a shill at the gaming tables of the Cowboy Bar in Jackson. It was a sad ending for a gallant man who had led a bold and courageous life. He had worked hard and been successful. Still, circumstances beyond his control brought him down, as they did so many others in the nation.

Si Ferrin died in 1944 at the age of seventy-one. His widow, Edith, continued to play an important role in Jackson Hole's history until her death in 1974 at the age of eighty-nine. Despite Si's final financial difficulties, his family certainly flourished. When Edith died,

Top: The Ferrin family home at 141 East Pearl Avenue in Jackson. The building still stands and has been home to a local business for twenty-five years, n.d. Jackson Hole Historical Society and Museum, 1958.2386.001.

Bottom: Last herd of Ferrin cattle driven to Idaho, n.d. Jackson Hole Historical Society and Museum, 2005.0045.011.

she and Si had 157 living descendants in four generations of children, grandchildren, great-grandchildren, and great-great-grandchildren. Their daughter Ada said of Si and Edith as parents, "I can never remember any one of us kids ever wanting for anything. Our folks saw to it that we all received good educations and we never had to go without anything we really needed."

When Si's first wife, Emmeline, died, she was buried in the South Park Cemetery because the Jackson cemetery was not started until a few years later. Si and Edith Ferrin are buried as they requested, with Emmeline in South Park.

CHAPTER FOUR

THE BURT FAMILY

ARRIVED IN JACKSON HOLE IN 1908

⊱⊶⊙⊷⊰

IN the early summer of 1908, a young man came to the top of Teton Pass from Idaho. The view of Jackson Hole from the summit was so breathtaking that it changed his life. "I took one look, and I've been here ever since," he wrote nearly forty years later. That one look was a good thing for Jackson Hole, for this was Struthers Burt, and he would become a key player in some of the valley's historic events.

As a member of a wealthy Philadelphia family, Burt had a background that presented a sharp contrast compared to most of the other homesteaders in the valley: he was a highly educated, sophisticated man of the world who had graduated from Princeton University and had studied at a German university and at Oxford University in England. His family wanted him to become a banker or a lawyer, but he wanted to become a writer. He compromised temporarily by teaching English at Princeton—and then the West called to him. Perhaps the call resonated with the lives of a couple of his ancestors who were not bankers or lawyers—his uncle, who was a cattleman in Arizona, and his great-grandfather, who was a fur trader in Wyoming's Green River area in the 1830s. Burt was twenty-six years old when he went West to stay.

His plan was to become a dude rancher who was also a writer. He became a partner in Jackson Hole's first dude ranch, the JY, but soon fell out with his partner, whom he designated as "a sort of financial Blue Beard." He left with Dr. Horace Carncross, the JY's physician, to homestead their own dude ranch. The odds were against them. "An unrecorded wit has said that homesteading consists of the government betting you one hundred and sixty acres against starvation, and the government always winning," Burt wrote in his famous book *The Diary of a Dude-Wrangler*, adding, "In the main this is true." It was true indeed for some homesteaders in Jackson Hole, but not for Struthers Burt and Horace Carncross. Their dude ranch, the Bar BC—for Burt and Carncross—became one of the most famous dude ranches in the Rocky Mountain West. It was the star in Jackson Hole's golden age of dude ranching and colorfully represented a way of life that still influences the valley's identity today.

Still, it should not have worked. Two greenhorns set out in the late summer of 1911 to find a suitable location for their dude ranch. Their entire capital was $2,000, most of it borrowed. And they were two quirky characters: "Almost every day we would get on our horses and

Struthers Burt was supposed to become a banker or lawyer. Instead, he chose to become a dude rancher and writer. He was successful as both, n.d. Jackson Hole Historical Society and Museum, 1958.0275.001.

ride until sundown, exploring out-of-the-way corners of the valley," Burt wrote. "We argued and fought endlessly. We have done that ever since, but always with infinite mutual respect and forbearance. The doctor is a conservative man and sees the worst side of things first; I am just the other way about. Sometimes we have fought for days over a five-foot jog in a fence. But this combination of opposing qualities makes for a good partnership. Frequently in the end our final half-and-half conclusion is not so far from being right."

The place they selected by the Snake River had grazing land and trees for building and for firewood; it had excellent hunting and fishing—and it had a fabulous location below a ridge that kept the ranch secluded, but was low enough to leave clear a spectacular view of the Tetons. It was a great choice, and time would prove them right.

Over the winter, they prepared. They ordered supplies for things they could make on site. For the things they could not make, Burt pored over the "Western Bibles"—two massive catalogs from two huge mail-order houses—and checked off what they needed "from adzes to zithers." At the end of the winter he claimed he could repeat those catalogs backwards and forwards. They recruited the help they would need for their first season, and then they went back East to recruit fifteen dudes. When they returned to Jackson Hole, they had May and June in which to get everything ready.

"In that time," wrote Burt, "out of sage-brush and deadfall, we would have to create a home for 15 Eastern people and the five or six Westerners needed to take care of them, and not only a home for the former but a comfortable and artistic one as well, a very different matter from starting an ordinary ranch. Moreover, having taken care of the interiors of our guests and the interiors of our cabins, we would have to turn our attention to the outside world and see that there were cows to milk and horses to ride and other horses to do the hauling and farm work . . . We would have to have at least seven small sleeping-cabins, fourteen by sixteen, with fireplaces, four bunkhouses, a couple of storehouses, a meat-house, corrals and necessary fencing, a well, and a large central cabin, the last with a kitchen, a dining-room, a sitting-room, and two or more smaller rooms for writing and card-playing." "In short," Burt concluded, "we had to build a small town in the wilderness, complete and self-sustaining in every detail." In just two months.

Amazingly, they pulled it off. The first dude at the Bar BC dined on canned fruits, coffee, beans, and carrots, while cabins were being completed. On record, he did not complain, "but ate his bad food contentedly and slept on the ground, and made friends immediately." Twelve years later Burt could write, "We built for fifteen people—we have been enlarging ever since."

All those scrambling efforts to build the Bar BC notwithstanding, Struthers Burt still found time to get married during this period. At Oxford in 1910 he had met Katharine Newlin, like himself an independent spirit and writer from a wealthy Eastern family. Katharine first came to the Bar BC as his fiancée in 1912. A long railroad trip to Idaho

Opposite page: Struthers Burt in ranch gear during the early days of the Bar BC dude ranch, c. 1920. Jackson Hole Historical Society and Museum, 1999.0054.001.

Right: Katharine Newlin married Struthers Burt in 1913. Like him, she became a prominent writer. Together, they created one of Jackson Hole's most colorful dude ranches, n.d. Jackson Hole Historical Society and Museum, 1958.0276.001.

plus three days by horse-drawn wagon over the Tetons to the ranch did not deter her. She returned to the Bar BC the next year as his bride and later gave birth to their two children at the ranch. Together, Struthers and Katharine Burt formed the unique character of the Bar BC that attracted so many individuals who shared their background. Struthers ran the dude ranch, Katharine wrote novels. She wrote over thirty books, several of which were made into Hollywood movies. One consequence was that the Bar BC attracted important literary figures from both the East and West Coasts. When yet another dude's typewriter was unloaded, one of the cowboys laughed and said, "That's the eighth typewriter on the ranch."

Still, one marvels that the dudes came. They faced a long, arduous, and expensive trip to a remote, rustic, and expensive dude ranch that featured pit toilets, portable tin tubs for bathing, no electricity, simple food, and no nearby amusements for the evenings. Robert Betts, a New York advertising executive, who became so attached to Jackson Hole that he built a home in the valley and then wrote a book about its history, suggests that they came for the same reason he did, "and gladly, because dude ranches filled a previously unseen need by giving city dwellers a chance to shed their city ways and get out into some of the world's wildest and most beautiful country. Many Easterners became so taken with both the West and Westerners they returned year after year, usually to the same ranch, where they were treated as members of the family and expected to accept the vicissitudes of ranch life without complaint or have a timetable of east-bound trains thrust into their hands."

One celebrated case in point is the story of the Bar BC and the Countess of Flat Creek, as she became known locally. She was Cissy Patterson, heiress to a huge Eastern newspaper fortune and a Polish countess by marriage. She divorced the count and came West. She arrived, mud-splattered, at the Bar BC after dark and on a wet night, accompanied by her daughter, a maid, and seven trunks. The Burts and

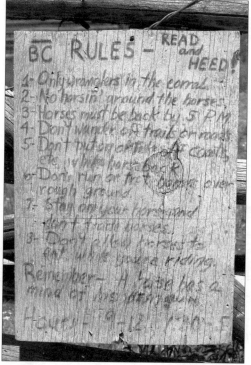

Top: One of the Bar BC's popular costume parties, n.d. Jackson Hole Historical Society and Museum, 1958.2014.001.

Left: Bar BC western rules for eastern dudes, c. 1920. Jackson Hole Historical Society and Museum, 1958.0585.001.

Dr. Carncross were throwing a fancy-dress party in the main cabin, and the first person the countess met was her hostess, Katharine Burt, who said, "Hello, I'm a cavewoman."

As longtime Jackson Hole dude rancher Jack Huyler tells the story,

> Mrs. Patterson informed her that she would like a bath drawn immediately and supper served in her cabin. When she recovered from shock, Mrs. Burt told her new guest firmly that she could find a zinc washtub hanging on an outside wall of her cabin; inside the cabin, a bucket of water and a Yellowstone stove with which to heat it. Furthermore, supper was served only in the dining room and that was soon. The bath would have to wait. Mrs. Patterson turned and called to her maid, Abigail, to unpack nothing as they were leaving in the morning. Mrs. Burt countered with the information that after a pull such as today's, the team needed, and would have, a day of rest. They could leave the day after tomorrow.

The following morning, having experienced the Bar BC atmosphere in daylight, Cissy Patterson sent her maid back East with six of the seven trunks. She and her daughter stayed. She and Katharine Burt became good friends, and when she bought herself a ranch in Jackson Hole, Cissy took the Bar BC's colorful cowboy Cal Carrington with her to run it. She should have been completely out of place in Jackson Hole; instead, she became one of this valley's best-liked dudes and part-time residents. The local lore is that Cissy was an expert in the art of cussing. The driver of the stagecoach that carried people over the pass, himself adept at the art, once said that Cissy was the only person he ever let talk to his horses when they needed talking to. "I owe her much," he said with admiration. "She didn't teach me all I knew in talking to horses, but she sure as hell gave me a few wonderful new ideas." Like early homesteader Lucy Shive, Cissy Patterson was liked for being the woman she was, unafraid to live and speak as she saw fit. This was an attribute that helped form the character of Jackson Hole.

Dude ranches flourished in the 1920s during what became known as the golden age of dude ranching. Americans, increasingly with their own automobiles, had discovered their own country—and particularly the West—as a desirable destination for holidays. Those who preferred to come West by train were lured by the Union Pacific with brochures like this: "*Dude Ranches Out West*: Dawn flaming over the hills in a

The flamboyant Cissy Patterson, formerly the Countess Eleanor Gizycka, was a favorite dude at the Bar BC. When she bought her own Jackson Hole ranch, she became known affectionately as the Countess of Flat Creek, n.d. Jackson Hole Historical Society and Museum, 1958.3401.001.

sighing, beckoning wilderness of spruce and pine—the refreshing bab-
ble of a tumbling mountain brook—neighing horses—ravishing aroma
of bubbling coffee and crisping bacon—would you like to wake up and
discover all this?"

The rise of dude ranches also coincided with what one historian
calls "America's elevation of the cowboy, arguably America's most emi-
nent folk hero . . . Western dress mimicked cowboy garb." Struthers
Burt agreed. "And what a beautiful and romantic dress the cowboy costume is at that!" he wrote. "Spanish in derivation, American in adapta-
tion . . . big spurs, high-heeled boots, covered with fancy stitching,
'chaps' of leather or angora wool, flannel shirt, neck handkerchief, and
sombrero. The one national costume we have."

Put it all together and it is not surprising that another historian
rated the dude ranch as "the single most unique contribution of the
Rocky Mountain West to the ever-growing national vacation industry."

The Bar BC played a major part in the rise of dude ranches in
Jackson Hole; indeed, it could rightly be called a major cause of this
rise. By 1924, Struthers Burt had become dude ranching's most articulate spokesperson, and when his extremely popular memoir, *The Diary
of a Dude-Wrangler*, appeared in the *Saturday Evening Post* and also in
book form, it inspired a whole new generation of dude ranchers and
dudes. The Bar BC had "grown like a mushroom in wet weather," as
Burt put it, and had become a social center and a major employer in
Jackson Hole. The comings and goings of its dudes were reported regularly in the local newspaper.

The Bar BC's staff decidedly added to the western glamour of the
ranch. Here is Burt's portrait of the Bar BC cook: "She was a magnificent woman—this cook, and in her youth she must have been very
beautiful. She had a charming way of sitting on the edge of a table and
suddenly lifting up her skirt and producing from her stocking a bag of
Bull Durham and some papers and rolling herself a cigarette. She
had come West on her honeymoon in a covered wagon and once,

Top: In terms of location, the Bar BC had it all. It lay nestled in its solitude below a bench that caused the glorious Teton Range to look even closer than it was. The log cabins lay near the ranch's own freshwater pond, and a short walk took dudes to the Snake River for floating or fishing. Photo by Harrison Crandall. Jackson Hole Historical Society and Museum, Harrison Crandall Collection, 1958.2440.001. Bottom: Dudes of all ages enjoyed the Bar BC pond, which was fed by a nearby creek, n.d. Jackson Hole Historical Society and Museum, 1958.0293.001.

while her husband was away from camp, had stood off three desperadoes by herself."

And here is his portrait of the chief cowboy: "He chose his own name and taught himself to read and write when he was about 35 years old. Starting with nothing at all, he has by now acquired two profitable ranches, and during the winter indulges a taste for traveling. Not long ago a famous motion-picture actress patronized him in the following manner, and received the following answer. The blond-haired screen star was doing a Western and was on location in the valley, and was being very kind and gracious, indeed, to all 'the dear simple people.' Having heard that the proper way to address a native when first meeting him was to ask him how he had wintered, she asked Nate. 'Fine,' he replied. 'I wintered in Paris, Berlin, and Rome.' "

By this time, Struthers Burt had achieved what he set out to do as a young man: he was both a successful dude rancher and a successful writer. During the 1920s he wrote thirty-seven short stories that were

Supplanting horses and wagons, this Bar BC Model T truck carried dudes and supplies to and from Idaho across Teton Pass, 1930s. Jackson Hole Historical Society and Museum, 1958.0202.001.

published in prestigious magazines. One story won the coveted O. Henry Award First Prize for best short story by an American writer (beating F. Scott Fitzgerald, who received Second Prize). As he grew older, Burt shifted to novels and became a best-selling novelist.

Struthers Burt once described himself this way: "The dude-wrangler is a ranch owner, a cowman, a horseman, a guide, a wholesale chambermaid, a cook, and storekeeper rolled into one." In his definitive study of the creation of Grand Teton National Park, historian Robert Righter adds "conservationist" to this description: "Of all the early settlers in Jackson Hole, it was the dude-wrangler who understood the value of the big game and the natural beauty . . . . And in his own mind, he already knew that the future of Jackson Hole lay not in livestock, agriculture or timber, but in tourism: tourism not based on gaudy dance halls, gambling or liquor, but one centered on a comfortable but close relationship with nature . . . . To accomplish this end Jackson Hole had to remain natural and unspoiled." Already, a threat to an unspoiled Jackson Hole had been steadily mounting. By the early 1920s the threat was ominous indeed. As he had been a leading spokesperson for dude ranching, Struthers Burt now became a leading spokesperson for conservation.

The threat was a double whammy, a possibility that is stunning to contemplate as one visits Grand Teton National Park today. There was a secret plan to construct a dam on the outlet of Jenny Lake. This dam would have raised the water level of Jenny Lake by twenty feet and the level of Leigh Lake by ten feet. A small group of Jackson Hole residents were aghast and sought to block the project. "They were going to dam one of the near-by lakes," Burt wrote, "incidentally ruining the lake, a lake which is as beautiful as any in the world." There was also a plan to dam the Gros Ventre River, the Buffalo River, and Spread Creek, the three most important Snake River tributaries in the valley. There was yet another plan to dam Emma Matilda Lake and Two Ocean Lake. All of this for the profit of developers who intended to sell the water to

Idaho farmers. Finally, the Forest Service planned to issue permits for logging on the shores of Jackson Lake and for the opening of several mines in the valley. As the great naturalist Olaus Murie concluded in his book about Jackson Hole, "Here were threats to the natural condition of all the main lakes and streams of the valley, and a threat to the floor of the valley itself."

And there was more. The valley floor was also under threat from commercial development aimed at the tourist trade. Along the Jenny Lake road, construction of tourist facilities raced ahead. In addition to gas stations, cheap cabins, and hot-dog stands, there were also a dance hall, a billboard advertising a local ranch as "the Home of the Hollywood cowboy," the rusting bodies of junked automobiles, and a ramshackle rodeo arena. This was in the Bar BC's neighborhood, so Struthers Burt had an up-close view. He did not like it. "This speedway down here," he wrote, "the El-Bo Ranch and the south end of Timber Island, not to mention Jenny's Lake, has about sickened me with this neck of the woods."

Burt had been one of Horace Albright's most articulate and formidable opponents when Albright wanted to include part of Jackson Hole in Yellowstone National Park. He was now about to change his mind. During the winter of 1922, Albright got a phone call from his former opponent, who said, "You know, we were wrong. We can't go on the way we are. I think the park is the thing to have. I'd like to come over to your side."

This decision by Struthers Burt was extremely important to the future of Jackson Hole, for he took a leading role in the fight to establish Grand Teton National Park. "In fact," concludes Robert Righter, "an argument can be made that without his efforts, the park as we know it today would not exist."

"The Battle of Jackson's Hole," as Burt called the struggle for the park, was an ongoing drama with a cast of characters that pitted major Jackson Hole residents against each other. The battle also included two

U.S. Presidents, a multimillionaire philanthropist, and a Hollywood movie star. While neighboring Yellowstone National Park took only two years from idea to realization, Grand Teton National Park took fifty-two years. The fight in Jackson Hole was so acrimonious, Olaus Murie sadly reported, that "card parties, dinner parties had their embarrassments if certain ones on 'the other side' were present. In some inexplicable way an atmosphere was created in which one felt inhibited from even mentioning the subject. There was no such thing as getting together and talking it over."

But a notable event occurred in this battle in the summer of 1923. It is commemorated by a bronze plaque on Maud Noble's cabin by the Snake River in Moose. At the meeting in her cabin were Struthers Burt and Horace Carncross, representing the dude ranchers; veteran rancher Jack Eynon; veteran homesteader and then Jackson businessman J. R. Jones; newspaper owner Dick Winger; and Yellowstone Park superintendent Horace Albright. Veteran rancher Si Ferrin was supposed to have joined them. His fellow rancher spoke for him and said what he would have said, if he could have been there. As historian Robert Righter describes the scene, these six men and Maud Noble "pulled their chairs around the fireplace (for Maud enjoyed a fire even in the summer) to discuss the fate of the pristine valley they all loved."

They came up with the Jackson Hole Plan, and decided they needed a wealthy benefactor to implement it. Jack Eynon and Dick Winger traveled east and returned without financial backing. The plan seemed dead. Then John D. Rockefeller, Jr., took his family west and came to Jackson Hole on a vacation. The rest, as they say, is history and has been fully detailed by several historians. Here are some of the dramatic high points.

Mr. Rockefeller became deeply inspired by the Tetons, which he described as "quite the grandest and most spectacular mountains I have ever seen . . . a picture of ever-changing beauty which is to me beyond compare." He agreed to buy out all the private lands north of Jackson

Above: Mr. and Mrs. John D. Rockefeller, Jr., picnicking in Grand Teton National Park, 1931. National Park Service, Grand Teton National Park.

Opposite page, top: Dudes from the Bar BC rode the ranch stagecoach to the Elbo Rodeo, where they participated in various events or rooted for the Bar BC cowboys, c. 1925. Jackson Hole Historical Society and Museum, 1958.1192.001.

Opposite page, bottom: Maud Noble's cabin in Moose, where Struthers Burt and other leading Jackson Hole citizens met in the summer of 1923 and formulated the Jackson Hole Plan to preserve the valley from commercialization, 2005. Photo by Charles Craighead. Jackson Hole Historical Society and Museum, 2005.0125.002.

and Spring Gulch and to donate them to the National Park Service, and in 1927 he financed a company that would buy the lands. As it turned out, he had a long wait between buying and donating those lands.

The final say in the creation of Grand Teton National Park had to come from Congress, so Struthers Burt went national in his exhortations. He published a major article, "The Battle of Jackson's Hole," in the influential magazine, *The Nation*, arguing that conserving natural resources was a necessity for the country; that space, solitude and fresh air were a necessity for human beings; and that therefore "the eyes of all those interested in conservation are today turning toward this small mountain valley—this Jackson's Hole—where one of the first decisive battles of conservation will be fought out."

By 1942, John D. Rockefeller, Jr., who had paid taxes on his properties for fifteen years without seeing any park materializing, grew impatient. He wrote a letter to Secretary of the Interior Harold L. Ickes in which he suggested that if the federal government did not want his gift of land or could not arrange to accept it, he might consider selling it to private buyers. The letter was intended to provoke action at long last, and it succeeded. On March 15, 1943, President Franklin D. Roosevelt signed an Executive Order. "Jackson Hole Monument was now a fact," wrote historian John Daugherty, "a 221,000-acre addition to the national park system."

The reaction in Jackson Hole was volatile. One of the more colorful responses came from a small group of ranchers headed by seventy-six-year-old Peter Hansen and his son Cliff, who decided to call public attention to their cause against the Monument. They organized a protest cattle drive across Monument lands to their summer range. As Cliff Hansen tells the story, "We got Wallace Beery, a well-known movie star who enjoyed many friends here and had wide recognition nationally, to ride with us." Beery was so overweight that they had trouble getting him mounted on Cliff's sister's horse. Once in his saddle and ready for action, Beery, true to his Hollywood background, laid a rifle across the pommel, pushed back his hat, and told Cliff, "When you want your picture taken, put your hat back so the sun will shine in your face and they see you." The protest got a double spread in the center of *Time* magazine, and other national media picked up the story.

Over time, as tempers settled and the serious concerns of local officials were dealt with, there was a local shift in favor of the park. The changing attitude of Cliff Hansen, later Governor of Wyoming and U.S. Senator from Wyoming, is symbolic of this switch. Hansen was never a fervent conservationist, but he did come to accept the value of Grand Teton National Park. And he was always a fair-minded man:

> When I was Governor, I went back to the World's Fair in New York City, and the Rockefellers entertained me at a very nice luncheon. There were about 30 people present, as I recall. I said that I had been against Park extension tooth and nail but that I couldn't have been more wrong. This area has the beauty and the uniqueness to make it something that stands alone, and I said that it deserved to be a national park. That was a full 180 degree turn for me. I have said to the Rockefellers on many occasions that we are very grateful they had the perception and benevolence they demonstrated.

Just for the official record, and for a happy ending: in 1949, after six years of local and legislative attacks against it, the Jackson Hole Monument controversy was settled. John D. Rockefeller, Jr., finally felt confident that the land would become part of Grand Teton National Park and conveyed his gift of 33,562 acres of Jackson Hole land to the United States government and its citizens. In 1950, Grand Teton National Park as we now know it was finally established. A plaque commemorating Mr. Rockefeller's crucial part in this piece of history sits on Lunch Tree Hill above Jackson Lake Lodge, where the Tetons first inspired him.

Struthers Burt, who had fought so well for the park, lived to see it finally established. But before that time he had stopped being a dude wrangler. By 1930, both he and Katharine Burt had become very successful authors and wanted to turn to write full-time in their later years. They sold the Bar BC, which eventually became part of Grand Teton National Park, and moved to the Three Rivers Ranch on Pacific Creek. From there, they continued to be active members of the Jackson Hole community they had so signally helped to create.

When Struthers Burt died peacefully at age seventy-two in the Jackson hospital in 1954, the local paper expressed the loss felt by the community: "On Saturday, Jackson Hole lost one of its most distinguished and best-loved citizens . . . While Mr. Burt had wide interests and national repute, he still entered whole-heartedly into every activity for the betterment of Jackson's Hole and the preservation of its outstanding scenic charms, and was a loyal citizen in whom the community had great pride." When Katharine Burt died at age ninety-five in 1977, the speaker at her memorial service said, "To remember Katharine Newlin Burt this afternoon is to recall vintage Jackson Hole." Struthers Burt is buried in the Aspen Hill Cemetery in Jackson, next to his wife and daughter. In his own words, this might well be his epitaph:

You must search for the loveliness of America;
it is not obvious; it is scattered;
but when you find it, it touches you
and binds you to it like a
great secret oath taken in silence.
I wish that it were possible for me
to see the Rockies once more for the first time.

CHAPTER FIVE

THE FEUZ FAMILY

ARRIVED IN JACKSON HOLE IN 1911

A surprisingly large proportion of early Jackson Hole settlers were immigrants from foreign countries. They came from Canada and from all over Europe. In the fall of 1910, one young immigrant from Switzerland saw Jackson Hole for the first time. He came from a tiny village high in the Swiss Alps, where his family had lived since 1547. He was an expert mountain climber and guide, and he was homesick for his native mountains. When he found the Tetons, he found the home his heart hungered for. Although his family had already moved twice since arriving in the West, he persuaded his wife to move one last time. They homesteaded in Jackson Hole in 1911. They were Gottfried (Fred) and Caroline Feuz, and this is their story.

Fred Feuz was born in 1877 in Gsteigwiler, an 800-year-old village on a steep mountainside at the foot of three of Europe's most famous Alps: the Eiger, the Mönch, and the Jungfrau. It is difficult to imagine more heart-rending circumstances than those of Fred's family. In her short life, his mother gave birth to twelve children, and six of them died, five within a few months of being born. She died soon after the death of her twelfth child. At age sixteen, Fred, the oldest surviving child, became the caretaker of his five younger siblings. The most likely explanation for this mournful situation is that Fred's mother suffered from chronic tuberculosis, a common disease at that time; and as she nursed her babies, they would contract the disease from her. Only the strongest survived.

The family was poor. Fred's father made his living by mountain climbing and guiding in the summers; during the long, hard winters he chopped and delivered firewood that he sold to villagers. Fred helped his father with the wood, and he also took any odd jobs he could find in order to help support the family. He had to take time out to go to school because Swiss law decreed that all children attend school for nine years or their parents could face prison. Every morning before school, Fred made sure that his brothers and sisters had their breakfast; immediately after school, he hurried home to cook, clean, and take further care of them.

The Eiger and Mönch summits above Fred Feuz's home village in Switzerland, 1998. Photo courtesy of Bill Koopman.

When he was old enough, he studied hard to pass the rigorous qualifications to become a mountain guide and climbing instructor. He guided climbers up the Eiger, Mönch, and Jungfrau, and as far away as the Matterhorn near the Italian border. In the winter, he guided climbers on the north face of the Eiger, where they trained for summer climbs of Mount Everest. He got his only real vacation in his early twenties, when he was caught in a rock avalanche and had to spend many months in a hospital. This gave him the opportunity to rest and do a lot of reading, and to meet people from beyond his village.

He was working as a climbing guide and instructor at a hotel in Grindelwald when he met Caroline Durtschi, and they fell in love. After Fred's painful youth with its poverty and its enormous responsibilities, Caroline must have felt like a ray of warm sunshine in his life. Where he had known misery and poverty, she had known joy and plenty. She was born in 1883 into a large family who owned a successful farm and a beautiful old home. The Durtschis had a rich family life that included working together on the farm and playing music together in the evenings. Caroline had a happy childhood and early on showed the cheerfulness and sense of humor that would grace her whole life.

When Caroline finished her Swiss schooling, she chose to go to France to a school for fine sewing, and to learn the French language. Her ambition was to work in the Swiss hotel field, and for this she needed one more language than her native German. Her family helped her to stay in France for two years, and her brother helped her buy a Singer sewing machine, imported from New York. This dependable and widely traveled sewing machine was a joy in her life and would become a trusted means of sewing for her family and for needed income when she and Fred homesteaded in Jackson Hole. Surprisingly, her parents emigrated first.

Why do people choose to emigrate to a foreign country? For most people, it is probably to seek a better life. But Caroline's family already had a very good life. They had every reason to remain in Switzerland, where they had centuries-deep roots and an old and profitable farm that they loved. Why would her parents, in their mid-fifties, leave all this and travel far away to a foreign land where they would have to start over again and learn a new language?

This is what made them do so. In 1905, young Swiss men who had emigrated to Utah and had become members of the LDS Church came back to their homeland as missionaries. Caroline's mother and sister joined first. Her father was not very interested in converting to Mormonism, but his brother had joined the Church and moved to Utah, so he freely gave the missionaries a bed and a good meal whenever they were in the neighborhood. This hospitality did not please the local Lutheran clergyman, schoolmaster, and villagers. The Durtschi's youngest son, John, was only about eleven years old and was in the village school. After taunting him about his family's interest in Mormonism, the schoolmaster beat John with a cane and threw him out of the school. The bruises from his beating caused John's eyes to swell shut. That did it. In outrage, Caroline's father and mother pulled up roots and moved their family to Utah.

This move left newlyweds Fred and Caroline without their major family support. They lived in what their oldest daughter later called "a lean-to to a lean-to" on Fred's family home. The lean-to was small and inadequate. Because the village was in the shadow of a big mountain, the lean-to was also dismally dark. Fred's work took him away from home for weeks at a time; and, hard as they both worked, they could barely survive. Soon, they had two infant daughters. Caroline was housebound, taking care of the children, and often sewed all night long for a meager income. Meanwhile, her beloved family sent happy letters from Utah, describing their new farm and their many opportunities in the small, predominantly Swiss, community of Midway.

Those first years of marriage were very difficult. Caroline wrote, "We talked and we quarreled about moving many, many times." Even though Fred's two brothers had also emigrated to this country and wrote their own encouraging letters, he refused to move. Then his hand was forced. He was an expert hunter, and in order to keep his family fed he would shoot game. In most European countries at that time, all wild game belonged to the King or the nobles. In Switzerland, which did not have an aristocracy, the game was reserved for wealthy tourist hunters. Authorities caught Fred poaching a deer. The penalty was a fine of seven hundred francs or a year in prison, and sometimes both. There was no way Fred could pay the fine, and with him in prison his family would starve. That left only one final alternative: emigration. According to Feuz family history, Switzerland was running out of land for its population, and people without land or money were strongly invited by their government to leave the country for good.

And so in May of 1909, Fred and Caroline packed up her sewing machine, accordion, and his Swiss army rifle, and a few other belongings including their feather-filled bedding, and set out for Midway, Utah. They went first by train through France, then spent two weeks crossing the Atlantic on a small ship, and passed through Ellis Island and the shock of the English language barrier. Then it was another week across country by train with minimal food, during which time Caroline was continually sick from her pregnancy. Finally, in Salt Lake City, came the joyous reunion with their family, and soon the birth of their third child, in Midway.

Fred quickly found jobs with his brother-in-law building a power plant near Heber City and then working in the Park City mines. Every Saturday, after working from dawn to sunset and camping out all week, the two men walked miles from their work site over the mountains to Midway and home. After spending a night with their families they walked back late Sunday. Caroline worked happily on the family farm while the children played with their new cousins, and they all learned English as quickly as they could.

With three small children, Fred and Caroline really needed a home of their own. Her two brothers had started farms in Teton Valley, Idaho, and wrote telling them about good opportunities for work and for acquiring land. Once more, everything was packed, and the young family moved. They settled into a small cabin near her brothers' farms. They did not own the cabin, but it was private. Once more, Fred worked at any job he could get and was often away for several months at a time. At home, Caroline planted a vegetable garden large enough to feed the family all year, and was helped by her brothers when needed. Soon, her parents sold their Midway farm and followed them to Teton Valley. Each family shared their bounty with the others. Fred, the best hunter among them, regularly returned from his hunts with meat for everyone.

It was on one of these hunting trips that he first saw Jackson Hole and the Teton Range. Dazzled by the view, he walked from the north to the south end of the valley, then from east to west, to see all the possibilities for homesteading. He chose 160 acres near Spread Creek and with his brother's help built a typical two-room homestead log cabin. For the first time in his life, Fred Feuz owned his own land, something he never could have achieved in Switzerland. This must have been quite a feeling for him.

For Caroline, the initial emotion was less jubilant. As their son Emil was fond of saying, while his Dad was busy looking *up* at the beautiful "American Alps," his mother, a farmer's daughter, was looking *down* at the rocky soil, covered with sagebrush.

On a bright September day, the family drove through golden aspen trees and saw their new home for the first time. Their oldest daughter, Lena, remembers, "To the children it was wildly exciting, a small unfinished log cabin sitting in the tall sage brush." She soon realized that, to their mother, it was a different experience. "I do remember coming from the bright outdoors into the small dark room, finding Mother tacking up a false ceiling of cheesecloth to the beams to keep the dirt on the roof from sifting into the room, and in answer to my questions about this, Mother laid down the hammer and burst into tears. That was the only time I ever saw her weep." Two weeks later, as Lena remembers it,

> We woke up to find a new baby, Albert, had arrived while we slept. Father left the second morning to drive the team to Victor to get winter supplies and most needed windows for the cabin. He had put off making this trip, waiting for the baby, and now it was high time. Winter was upon us in the shape of eight inches of new snow, and I remember Mother's tracks out toward the corral where she was milking the cows, while I had been told to watch the children, new baby and all, and above all to keep stuffing wood into the kitchen range. How surprised Father was when he came home and found that the little stove had consumed over half the wood he had cut for the winter, heating the windowless cabin.

Fred and Caroline Feuz by the kitchen table in their home on the ranch, 1940. Jackson Hole Historical Society and Museum, 1993.4993.065.

After that first hard winter, Fred and his brother Pete built a room and a half onto the cabin. They also built all the furniture. Caroline made quilts and curtains on her faithful Singer sewing machine. Large coffee cans filled with pink geranium blooms brought color inside the dark cabin. Fred secured irrigation water rights from the Buffalo Fork, they grubbed sagebrush, Caroline irrigated, and they planted their first garden and field. The children learned to milk and herd the cows, and Fred hunted and took any outside job he could get. It was a classic homesteading start in the difficult climate and terrain of Jackson Hole.

The Feuz family struggled on their homestead for many years, their hard times leavened by their optimism and dedication, with a special flavor added by their warm Swiss traditions. The Feuz's experience paints a good picture of early ranch life. What were the tasks they had to do, no matter what? How did they perform them? What were their joys, their pleasures? Was life good?

In Caroline's own words, from the Durtschi family history,

> It was work, work, work. Early in the mornings the children would wake up to my cooking breakfast on the old wood stove with Fred standing nearby, and we would happi-

The Feuz ranch—with homestead and outbuildings—was built slowly over the years, n.d. Jackson Hole Historical Society and Museum, 1992.4393.001.

ly discuss the upcoming day. It was the best time for us to visit and enjoy one another's company, following a good night's rest. Our plans were often frustrated by a lack of enough energy and too few tools to get everything accomplished which needed to be done. Each child was given a job according to age and ability. I tried to be a patient teacher, taking time to carefully point out to them the easiest way of doing their jobs. Fred and I made them feel it was a privilege to be allowed to help with all the necessary work.

Two outside tasks were essential and endless: irrigating the fields and removing the rocks. Irrigation ditches were dug with a horse pulling a plow so that water from Spread Creek could be used to irrigate the fields. Irrigating usually was Caroline's job. Here is her daughter's description: "All summer long Mother irrigated way into the night. The mosquitoes were fierce around dusk, so you had to stay inside until it got darker. I can see her yet, with her skirt tucked up around her waist. She wore high rubber boots that were almost always mismatched. They were covered with patches, and she wore a mosquito net around her head. She often had a shovel in hand. After she had fin-

ished irrigating the fields, she'd come in way after dark with the rest of the family sound asleep."

Each year they cleared more land. This involved moving the cobble rocks, which were everywhere. A new crop of rocks sprouted every spring, brought to the surface by the frost. The rocks had to be picked up by hand and tossed into the rock sled or along the rock borders by the buck and rail fences. This was usually the children's job, and some of these old rock piles can be found to this day.

Caroline talked Fred into planting alfalfa, an expensive investment, but it paid off in a greater yield at harvest time. They also harvested several wild meadows and sometimes leased other fields. Their cows produced well. They bought a few calves whenever they could, until they built a sizable herd.

At an altitude of over 7,000 feet and with a growing season of only about sixty days, Caroline planted a vegetable garden. Her garden survived such further odds as late frosts, after which everything had to be replanted, and local deer that happily ate whatever was growing. Still, the garden was a success, producing a good variety of vegetables.

"Winter nights, I sewed," Caroline said. "Not only for my family, but the little Singer was still sewing for neighbors for a bit of cash. I let my oldest daughter, Caroline Ida, stay up with me and read out loud while I sewed. We read our way through the Bible." Every single word. "Mother didn't want me to leave anything out," said her daughter. "I didn't mind, however. I so enjoyed this precious time alone with my Mother." As the other children grew older, each had special time alone with their Mother.

Meanwhile on those long, freezing winter nights, Fred was busy as well. Picture him perched on top of the haystacks at 40 degrees below zero, lying awake between his blankets and keeping watch. This was his method of keeping the herds of hungry elk from eating his hay. As one of his grandchildren proudly announced, "They soon learned not to tangle with Grandpa."

Drinking water was carried daily in buckets from the spring on the hill. A bucket of drinking water was always on the kitchen counter with a dipper ready to slake anyone's thirst. Hot water was always available in a special water well compartment in the woodstove. For washing dishes, two enamelware pans were filled with cold water and placed on the stove to heat while the family ate their meal. One pan was for washing, one for rinsing.

Water for cleaning and laundry was carried from an irrigation ditch near the back door. Laundry was done once a week and took all day. The kids hauled water from the ditch to be warmed in the kitchen. Clothes were scrubbed by hand with homemade soap, often made with bear grease, and put through a hand-cranked wringer for rinsing. The clean laundry dried on outdoor clotheslines, even in the winter when it froze. Clothes were ironed with two sadirons—heavy, double-ended flatirons that stood on the stove. A portable handle was fastened to one

"Our horses were truly wonderful," said Caroline Feuz. "They helped build up our place," n.d. Jackson Hole Historical Society and Museum, 2005.0045.015.

iron. When that one got too cold, the handle was switched to the other iron waiting on the hot stove. Torn clothing was always mended and socks darned, usually by the younger Feuz girls. Nothing was ever wasted.

They baked their own bread from their own wheat, which they ground themselves. This also took a full day every week. The old adage about "sweating over a hot stove all day" is a literal description of much work done by homestead women.

Fred often worked away from home, taking any available jobs to earn cash that was badly needed to buy farm machinery, seed, and supplies. He usually hired out his team along with himself. "Our horses were truly wonderful," said Caroline. "We owe those horse teams a debt of gratitude. Even though they were often mismatched teams, they helped build up our place, doing much of the heavy work." In the fall, Fred was a hunting guide. The long winter he used for trapping.

Family histories describe in detail the working life of Caroline's early Jackson Hole homesteading life. During the long, cold winter months, Caroline rose at 4:00 a.m. and went out with her lantern to the barn, where she raised chickens. She made an unusual but effective feed for them by mixing ground elk bones into their mash. This made her chickens lay eggs with hard shells during the winter months, when shells usually were too soft for eggs to be used. She charged $1.00 a dozen for her eggs, an outrageous amount at the time. But people paid it, because hers were the only eggs to be had. For Caroline, it was one more way she could earn needed cash.

She made butter in a wooden cylinder churn that was churned by hand. This was also a chore for the younger children (and later grandchildren), who were pressed into service at a young age. "We got to help and be part of the family labor force," said one granddaughter. "We were honored to be included." Being Swiss, Caroline also made cheese in wooden forms she had brought from Switzerland. Surplus milk, cream, butter, and cheese were sold and delivered to some of the neighboring ranches.

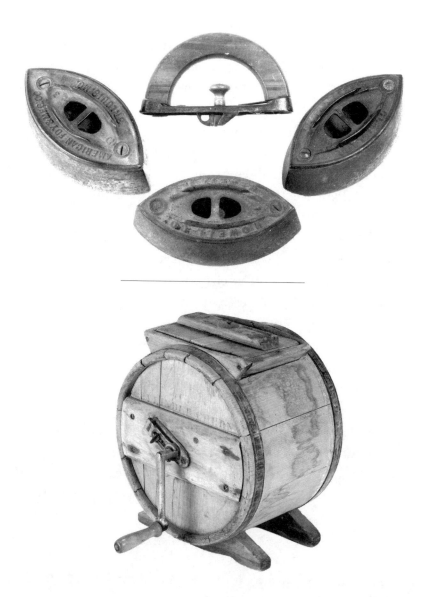

Top: Homesteaders used sadirons—heavy, double-ended flatirons—to press clothing. Irons were left on the hearth or stove to heat. The hot iron was lifted by the interchangeable handle. Photo by Latham Jenkins / CircumerroStock.com. Gift of Daisy Bernice Linn Tucker. Jackson Hole Historical Society and Museum, 2005.0123.001. Bottom: Homestead women churned butter by hand in churns much like this one. Photo by Latham Jenkins / CircumerroStock.com. Jackson Hole Historical Society and Museum, 1958.0931.001.

They always had plenty of meat—sage hens, rabbits, elk, and moose brought in by Fred. Everyone agreed that Caroline was an imaginative cook and that her stews and soups were always delicious.

Outside the window of their cabin, there was always a huge pile of wood with an ax nearby, ready for the never-ending chore of splitting firewood for cooking and heating.

Saturday night was bath time. The big metal washtubs that hung on a nail outside the house were brought down, and buckets of water were hauled from the ditch. The water was heated on the stove. This all took place in the kitchen, because it was the warmest room. Several kids shared one tub of water. In many early settlers' homes, one towel was shared by all; but in the Feuz home, their son Emil remembers that everyone had the luxury of their own bath towel.

There were no days off, except Sunday. Even though he was not affiliated with any church, Fred was adamant about resting on the Sabbath. "God wanted it that way," he claimed, "and besides people and animals both need the rest."

The family worked hard, and they also played whenever they had the chance. Fred got a wind-up gramophone, and their daughter Anna remembers her parents winding it up and playing a polka while dancing the schottische for their amused children. Fred would also bring out his accordion, and they often sang songs together in their home.

Christmas was special. "No matter how little money, there were always surprises," said daughter Lena. "Caps and mittens, even sweaters that Mother had knitted secretly after we slept. Sugar caramelized and broken up for candy, candles on the tree, the lamp extinguished and we all sang. Mother retold the Christ story and Father played the accordion. No, we did not know we were poor."

All their German neighbors were invited for Christmas dinner, a great feast. Caroline managed to get fresh oranges, a real treat in this remote area, and stuffed them into Christmas stockings. There were roasted apples and nuts, wonderful pastries, and plenty of fresh cream and butter. And always plenty of meat. Strings of popcorn and cran-berries decorated the Christmas tree Fred brought into the house. On Christmas Eve, candles were lit on the tree (with a bucket of water nearby in case of a fire) and the family and friends gathered around Fred and his accordion to sing their favorite traditional Christmas songs in German. Their favorites were "O Tannenbaum" (Oh, Christmas Tree) and "Stille Nacht" (Silent Night). It was a wonderful tradition that generations of the Feuz family remembered and wrote about.

Education was very important to Fred and Caroline, and they were willing to make major sacrifices so their children could go to school. Their oldest daughter tells how it was when she first went to school: "Early in June, Father put me back of himself on his gentle sad-dle horse and, after riding four miles, enrolled me in the school. Because of the rigorous winters, and the lack of good roads, school was only a summer term. The second morning, I hiked the distance alone to the little Wolff school house. Each term another sibling joined, and soon there were several of us hiking and enjoying school."

The Feuz children learned English at school and would daily take new words and phrases home for their parents to learn. Caroline wall-papered her teaching board with newspaper and would point out new words that they all practiced in order to improve their English. When school became a nine-month session, the children went by team and heated wagon, or they skied if the roads were impassable. When they got back from school, Caroline welcomed them with a hearty soup and fresh bread, and listened to their day's events before they started their chores. Fred, too, was interested in the children's education and served on the local school board for twelve years.

"Time passed," wrote Caroline. "First Lena and then Emma fin-ished the eighth grade. Because of the importance of education, it was decided that the girls would go to high school even though it meant they would have to leave home to do so. There was not yet a high school in Jackson and so heart-breaking good-byes were said as Lena, Emma, and then Ann were sent to Ashton, Idaho. They worked for their board and room and all finished high school." In fact, they all finished college and went on to productive careers away from home. The boys chose to stay home and ranch, eventually raising prime cattle on their ranches, some of which are still in the family today.

The family prospered. By the early 1930s, their new house had a kitchen, living room, and two bedrooms on the ground floor. Upstairs was a full loft with extra beds for whoever happened to be living there at the time. This came to include grandchildren, who were frequent visitors. Fred and Caroline built a spacious back porch onto the kitchen on the south side of the house. They had a small refrigerator connected to a butane tank outside. They never had electricity, a telephone, or indoor plumbing. Two outhouses sufficed the family for forty years.

Fred had begun to guide hunters, so the family decided to build four cabins as rentals for hunters and some summer tourists. Caroline cooked for them all. One hunter who had hunted for years with the family said that she was one of the finest cooks he had ever known.

With time came changes. The sons married and built their own ranches and homes in the valley. The daughters also married and lived far away from their parents. But with these changes came one of Fred and Caroline's greatest happinesses: grandchildren. There was hardly a time when one or more grandchildren weren't visiting. All of them remember their grandparents for their patience and good humor, and the old ranch as a very special haven.

Here is how one granddaughter recalled a typical evening at their home:

> They "dined" by the light of a kerosene lantern around the large oak table. One of my favorite memories of any mealtime at the Old Place was that, besides the good food, there was always great conversation going on while we ate.

Top: Early winter on the Feuz ranch, with Mount Leidy in the background, n.d. Jackson Hole Historical Society and Museum, 2003.0078.019.

Left: Fred and Caroline Feuz stand outside their home of many years, n.d. Jackson Hole Historical Society and Museum, 2003.0078.014.

Many topics were covered. The labors of the day, politics, etc., were all discussed. They seemed to energize one another with their enthusiasm for their work and interests. While the women were doing dishes, a small battery-operated Philco radio sat on the counter by the kitchen window. Nearby on the window sill were grandmother's blooms of pink geraniums growing from coffee cans. She definitely had a knack for adding some charm and color to the place. It was great to hear an old radio program or an orchestra playing some music. What a perfect way to end a hard day of work. The radio was really the only direct link to the "outside." It provided a unifying influence on rural Americans and especially helped immigrants like our family feel a part of their new nation.

Then came the time when John D. Rockefeller, Jr.'s company was buying up properties with the intention of donating them to what eventually became Grand Teton National Park. Times were economi-

cally hard, and many landowners were happy to sell. But not Fred and Caroline Feuz.

Both Fred's and Caroline's families were keen on family histories, and several histories were prepared and documented by family members over the years. At the Feuz family reunion in 1976, when she was seventy years old, Fred's and Caroline's daughter Lena presented *The Family History of Fred Feuz and Caroline Durtschi Feuz*. In it, she described her parents' struggle to keep their homestead.

"In 1928 great changes came over Jackson Hole," Lena wrote. "There were rumors of Park extension, neighbors sold out to a company which was secretly buying up ranches. It was very disquieting, there was no future, no certainty as to what to plan for. There were offers to buy the ranch, but these did not interest either of the Feuzes. They loved their land, it was their home."

By 1943 President Roosevelt declared the lands bought by Rockefeller's company a national monument. "We still refused to sell," Caroline Feuz related. "Finally, we were given a choice of either our property being confiscated, or trading for other land. The land they

A National Park Service ranger inspects an abandoned building on the Feuz ranch, n.d. Jackson Hole Historical Society and Museum, 2005.0045.013.

had in mind was bordering the end of the park near our son Walt's ranch. So we accepted this offer. The Park Service eventually had all our buildings and fences removed and burned."

Later, Caroline wrote in her diary, "For forty years we worked that place. There was never quite enough hours in the day or energy in our bodies to get all the work done that needed to be done, *but we did the best we could.*"

"After the painful decision to give up the place Father put his affairs in order," Lena reported in her family history. "Father had a final heart attack in August of 1951, and is buried in the Jackson cemetery, far from the land of his birth, but at home under his beloved Quaking Aspen. His love of nature and philosophy of life sustained him to the end."

A Jackson Hole newspaper obituary said of Fred Feuz,

> By his example he has shown all of us the reward of honest toil and a good life. He prospered and in so doing helped all others prosper. He was a good man and leaves a good name for his highly respected family. Our valley is a finer, better place in which to live because forty years ago a young Swiss pioneer thought no sight in all America quite so much reminded him of home as Jackson Hole and together with his family had the courage and will to make it their home. To his family goes the unspoken thanks and appreciation of an entire community who loved and cherished the friendship of Fred Feuz.

Caroline was left alone to make the move to the new place in Buffalo Valley. But before she made that move her brother came to visit with an old friend named Conrad Gertsch. This friend was one of the Swiss missionaries who had come back to stay with her family in Switzerland long ago, and who had first interested her in Mormonism.

He had married her cousin and was now a widower. He and Caroline decided to marry. She was baptized in the Mormon religion, and they were married in the temple in Idaho Falls. "Mother was so eager to embrace her new life that she left the now deserted old Feuz ranch without even taking the little Singer sewing machine," wrote Lena.

Caroline spent ten happy years with Conrad. The climate in Midway was gentler, she was surrounded by Swiss relatives and neighbors, and everyone welcomed her. This was the easiest time of her life. When she suffered a stroke in 1963, her niece took care of her. "It was a privilege, an absolute privilege," she said emphatically. Caroline died on August 31, 1963. She is buried on a hill in the Midway cemetery beside members of her Swiss family. She lived according to the motto and philosophy of life passed on to her by her mother: "Hope for the best, prepare for the worst, and gracefully take whatever comes."

Caroline Feuz in her later years, n.d. Jackson Hole Historical Society and Museum, 2003.0078.016.

The Feuz descendants still gather in Jackson Hole for an annual Fourth of July family picnic, an unbroken tradition since 1947. Fred and Caroline's granddaughter, Linda, wrote this epitaph for Fred and Caroline to commemorate their lives: "The story of Fred and Caroline Feuz is a twentieth-century story of an American immigrant family that were pioneers, settlers, ranchers, good neighbors, good citizens, parents, grandparents, and Christians. They did much more than just break sod and survive on their land. They thrived in their new world as well. The entire family possessed qualities of great industry, dignity, intelligence, physical strength, civility, and modesty. During the grueling years of 'just surviving' they never lost their sense of purpose, generosity or humor."

CHAPTER SIX

THE CHAMBERS FAMILY

ARRIVED IN JACKSON HOLE IN 1912

HEN Andy Chambers acquired the last homestead on Mormon Row in Jackson Hole, he joined a community with unique and inspiring roots in the West. Two of the founding families on Mormon Row had forebears who triumphantly survived extreme hardship and tragedy on the historic Mormon Trail.

The Mormons established the Mormon Trail in 1846 when they left Nauvoo, Illinois, to escape religious persecution and attacks on their people. The trail was long—almost 1,300 miles from Nauvoo to Salt Lake City. An estimated seventy thousand Mormon settlers traveled the trail from 1846 to 1869. Six thousand died on the trail.

Instead of following the Oregon and California Trails, the Mormons chose to create their own route. Travelers on the Mormon Trail improved it for the benefit of those who would follow, building a variety of permanent support facilities that included ferries. They planted crops and recorded pertinent information such as topography, distances, and types of terrain. Most of them traveled with wagons, but nearly three thousand Mormon pioneers traveled with handcarts that they pulled and pushed along the trail.

Among the pioneers who set out to travel the Mormon Trail during its early days were George and Hanna May and their family of seven children. The family's ocean voyage from their native England was harrowing, leaving them with no water and almost no food by the time they arrived in New Orleans. And worse was to come on land. On their way from New Orleans to the Mormon Trail, George May and two daughters died of cholera. Hanna May continued on with her remaining children. Then another son died, and finally Hanna died of consumption. Four teenage children were left. These orphans set out together on the four-month trek to Utah and arrived in Salt Lake City in October 1852. The oldest was James L. May, whose son James Ira May in 1896 became the first homesteader on Mormon Row or what was then known as Grovont. The area got its name because most of its settlers were Mormon.

Another founding Mormon Row homesteader was Thomas Alma Moulton, whose rustic barn has become an icon of western Americana. That the Moulton barn has survived is something of a miracle, but it is a greater miracle that Thomas Alma Moulton ever was born to build it.

His father, Charles Alma Moulton, was born on the Irish Sea as his family set out on their journey from England to Utah. The journey to the Mormon Trail was hard, but it was nothing compared to what awaited them on the trail. Here, the Moulton family of Thomas, Sarah, and eight children, including the tiny and frail baby Charles, became members of the Willie Handcart Company and thereby headed into one of the worst disasters in the entire history of the movement west.

The Willie Handcart Company left Camp Iowa on July 15, 1856—late in the season for its nearly thirteen hundred mile journey to Salt Lake City. By mid-September, the handcart travelers had only reached western Nebraska, and already their supplies were desperately low. At Fort Laramie, in eastern Wyoming, they found some meager provisions and decided to continue on to Salt Lake City, still five hundred miles away. In mid-October as they approached South Pass in western Wyoming, they were above 7,000 feet in altitude when severe snowstorms caught them. As temperatures dropped below zero and eighteen inches of snow fell on them, they were down to their last provisions. In the morning, before they struggled to drag their handcarts up over steep Rocky Ridge, they had to bury their dead in a snowdrift because the ground was frozen hard.

A truly heroic rescue mission saved the freezing and starving handcart survivors from certain death. In Salt Lake City, Brigham Young had heard of their desperate plight and immediately organized a massive rescue effort. Two hundred wagons with men and supplies went 250 miles out into fierce terrain and weather to save the stranded travelers. The rescuers found the Willie Company on October 21, one day after the surviving members had run out of food. More than seventy members of the company died on their ill-fated trip, but the rest finally reached Salt Lake City on November 9, 1856.

Miraculously, baby Charles survived the Willie Handcart Company disaster. He was so weak when he reached Salt Lake City that

A stone memorial at Rock Creek, Wyoming, commemorating the ill-fated 1856 journey of the Willie Handcart Company on the Mormon Trail, 2005. Photo by Zachary Larsen. Courtesy of the Riverton, Wyoming Stake.

no one expected him to live. Some people said that when he was held up to the sun, you could see right through his pitiful little body. But Charles not only survived, he grew up to father eleven children. The oldest of these children was Thomas Alma Moulton, who homestead-ed on Mormon Row in 1907, when he was twenty-four years old, and who built the Moulton barn.

Andy Chambers homesteaded right across from Thomas Alma Moulton in 1912. Like his neighbors on Mormon Row, Andy built a fine productive ranch out of a dry sagebrush plain. He was born in Eden, Utah, and left home when he grew tired of being broke and unable to find a job. "You couldn't buy a job down there," says his son Roy. "He said he came into this country with a dime. He liked the place so well because he was never broke after that."

Andy borrowed money to buy a team of horses so he could do the hard work of clearing and cultivating his 160 homestead acres. When he started to build his barn, he had trouble getting his log walls to stand up straight, so he went to his neighbor, Thomas Alma Moulton, for the best barn-building advice he could get. By 1916, Andy's homestead included an 18-by-20-foot log house which, like the T. A. Moulton Barn, still stands on Mormon Row. In the winters, Andy trapped coy-ote, mink, muskrat, and marten. According to Roy Chambers, "One coyote hide was worth $25. That was a hell of a salary for a month in those days."

Andy had been a bachelor on Mormon Row for five years when he met Ida Bell Kneedy, the Mormon Row schoolteacher, and not long afterward he followed a western tradition by marrying her. "If you go from Moran to Jackson," says Roy Chambers, "most all the old-timers there married schoolteachers. In fact, that was the way most of them found their wives."

Ida was born in Missouri and grew up in Kansas. Her mother died when she was six years old. Her father married again and moved the family to Jackson Hole, where he homesteaded north of Kelly, while

Top: Andy Chambers hard at work on his homestead, n.d. Jackson Hole Historical Society and Museum, 2003.0117.097. Bottom: The Andy Chambers homestead where Ida and Andy first lived, n.d. Jackson Hole Historical Society and Museum, 1958.1995.001.

Ida remained in Kansas to finish high school and Normal Training to become a teacher. After teaching school in Kansas for two years, she traveled west to join her family and got the job of teaching at the Grovont school on Mormon Row. "I was a real rookie schoolteacher," she said in her later years. "I didn't know much, but I learned."

Ida and Andy were both full of fun and ready for adventure. In February of 1918 they hitched Andy's sleigh and went across Teton Pass to Driggs, Idaho, to get married. Why go all the way across the pass in winter to do what they could have done in Jackson? "On account of my not being old enough," said Ida. "My Dad wouldn't give his consent. Andy thought he was going to have to go into the service right away. So we went out to Driggs and were married. That was February 23rd. I wasn't 21 years old until April."

"She always said the thing that attracted her to Andy was that he was different from anyone else she had ever met," Roy recalls. "In a community in those days you were known locally. But he was known from one end of the valley to the other because he was such a colorful character."

Andy had been right. Just a few months after their marriage he was called into the service. Ida stayed behind to take care of things while he was away. Things to take care of included hauling water from a nearby creek when it was running, and melting snow for water when it was frozen over. They also included learning to hitch a team of horses and plowing sixty acres for the grain crop that her neighbors helped her plant in the spring. And fencing the ranch in the summer when she closed the Grovont school, where she still taught.

All in all, things were well in hand at home when Andy returned from World War I. He and Ida continued ranching on the 160-acre homestead, purchasing another 160 acres to add to their holdings. Over the next twenty-seven years they operated their ranch, raising grain, cattle, and just about everything they ate. They also ran a post office, a store, and the mail route. And they brought seven children into the world. Ida was fond of saying, "The last time I ever wash a diaper, I'm going to raise it on a flag pole and fly it like a flag until it turns to shreds." Her sentiment resonated with many homestead wives and became widely quoted in the valley.

Most Jackson Hole homesteaders needed extra income in order to survive, and the Chambers family was no exception. One common source of income for women was operating post offices. The Mormon Row post office moved from home to home over the years, and from 1923 to 1935 Ida ran it out of her home. A postmaster's income was the money from the cancellation of stamps, and that could be as little as 30¢ a day. So Ida also ran a store from her home, with a gas pump outside. The two-story house was usually full of children beyond the seven in the family. The reason, says Roy Chambers, was that

The later Chambers home on Mormon Row in 1928, where Ida ran a store and the Grovont (Mormon Row) post office from 1923 to 1935. She also sold gas from a pump outside her home. Jackson Hole Historical Society and Museum, 1958.2826.001.

"Everybody thought it was fun to stay at the Chambers' because they seemed to have more fun than other people."

Andy had the Jackson-Moran mail contract from 1932 to 1940, a real boon during hard economic times. He ran the mail year-round, and in the summer he also raised hay and cattle on his homestead. During the Depression, when so many people were out of work, he produced enough from his land to care for five families.

Ranching on Mormon Row was no mean feat in the early days. The Row had some of the deepest and best soil in Jackson Hole, but it lacked water. The earliest Mormon Row settlers had to load their wagons with barrels and haul water from the Gros Ventre River for domestic use during all seasons and in the winter for livestock as well. Later, they had wells. This made the supply of water closer, but the water level was as much as 110 feet below ground, and the wells had to be hand-dug. Reaching water took a lot of arduous digging, reinforcing of walls so they would not cave in, and hauling dirt up to the surface. No one on Mormon Row had running water until 1927.

Major irrigation projects had to be built in the fields. The Mor-

Top: Digging ditches, and then dredging the ditches over and over again when they filled in, was the only way that most Jackson Hole homesteaders could irrigate their land, n.d. Jackson Hole Historical Society and Museum, Gift of the Snake River Ranch, 2003.0131.002. Left: Harvesting on Mormon Row, c. 1920. Jackson Hole Historical Society and Museum, 2005. 0127.001.

mon Row homesteaders dug a feeder ditch from the Gros Ventre River, and then they dug a network of irrigation ditches to their ranches. Many of these ditches can be seen in the area today. Using teams of horses, they dug ditches that they had to clear regularly by running a dragline through them. Roy Chambers estimates that it took twenty days to irrigate 160 acres with one stream of water.

As a further response to the lack of water, Mormon Row homesteaders became masters of the fine art of dry farming. This way of growing crops with a minimum of water served them well until the state built ditches to their properties in the late 1920s, and they could produce a wider variety of crops. Andy Chambers dry-farmed his land, raising grains like oats and wheat until 1927, when a new irrigation system made it possible to switch to raising cattle and hay.

When James I. May came to Mormon Row in 1896, he brought with him what was called the "ninety-day oat," so named because the growing season was only ninety days long. The ninety-day oat was Mormon Row's major crop for many years. The homesteaders got their harvest machinery slowly, and they shared it. James I. May's grandson Lanny remembers, "Even when I came along we were still sharing things. There were two thrash machines, then three thrash machines. The Chambers had a thrash machine, my grandfather had a thrash machine, and my uncle Clark Moulton had a thrash machine. So we managed to get all our thrashing done along Mormon Row."

All the women had big gardens that fed the families year-round. "You never did dare say you were bored," Roy recalls, "because the first thing you knew you had a hoe in your hand and you were in the garden." Everybody had root cellars. The Chambers family had one of the larger raspberry patches, and Ida put up about three hundred quarts of raspberries every year.

Some Mormon Row women were midwives, an important role in an isolated community. Thomas Alma Moulton's wife, Lucile, served as midwife for the births of at least twenty-two children on Mormon

Row, and she often stayed a few days after the birth of a baby to assist the mother with the other children.

The Mormon Row homesteaders built a school for their children, and sometimes included children from a neighboring community. The school had two rooms upstairs where the teacher lived, and two rooms downstairs where she taught. One of the girls who went through the eighth grade in the school reminisced, "We got a really good education because we got a lot of individual attention. And there was hardly ever anybody in the school that we weren't related to. So whenever someone would come, maybe a boy would come to go to school that we weren't related to, all the girls would get a crush on that boy because there were so few of them that weren't our brothers or our cousins."

Music was a large part of Mormon Row life. The homesteaders sang in the church they had built midway down the Row, and they held regular dances in the church. People brought their children and enough food to stay all night. Clark Moulton spoke fondly of the Saturday night dances:

> Recreation was the Saturday night dance twice a month or something. Veda's father had a violin and his boys could beat the drums and play the horns. Mel Chandler could play the piano. And sometimes they'd go as far as Jenny's Lake and sometimes they'd go to town and most of the time it was here in the old LDS church. People from Kelly would come, and of course you couldn't smoke or drink, but you could dance. We learned to dance, and we could dance, too. Everybody could dance, little fellas, big fellas, everybody learned to dance. The piano player would play until three o'clock in the morning and his fingers would be bleeding. He'd have to tape them.

Another source of fun centered around the rural telephone. Here is a story told by one Jackson Hole old-timer, John Ryan:

> Our telephones were those long, box-like types with a crank on one side and receiver on the other side and a mouth piece on the front, and everyone had their own ring, their identification. If you wanted to talk to Wilson, or someone over in Victor, central made the call and connected you with your party—listening in, of course, as we all did. It was enjoyed by all. We usually knew who was talking either by the ring or the voices. And we also knew some of the listeners. One lady had a clock on top of the telephone, and the ticking was clearly heard. Another had a baby who cried a lot, so we could identify her. Another was quite hard of hearing and would frequently ask to have something repeated. I remember Jack Eynon telling me about calling from up north in the valley to Fred Lovejoy down in Jackson, saying he had an important message to give him and would call back shortly after midnight. Needless to say, there was a lot of listeners in the valley that night that didn't get much sleep. It was a good joke enjoyed by all.

The valley also had its disasters. In 1925, without warning, the northern end of Sheep Mountain suddenly fell at great speed into Gros Ventre Canyon. In less than three minutes, over 20,000 cubic yards of rock slid into the canyon. The Gros Ventre slide was more than a mile long and one-half mile wide when it stopped. It dammed the Gros Ventre River, forming Lower Slide Lake and submerging cabins above the dam. People believed that the town of Kelly below the dam was in no danger. They were wrong. On May 18, 1927, water breached the natural dam, causing the catastrophic flood that wiped out Kelly and killed six people.

Ida Chambers lost her parents and brother in the Kelly flood. She had been concerned about the dam and had her parents come and stay with her on Mormon Row for several days.

But my Dad said, "There isn't [any] danger because there is no water behind the dam." See, at the time of the slide it hadn't built up to be dangerous. But when it did come, it was in the spring. Mr. Dibble had warned everyone that the slide was in danger of going out, and everyone had time enough to leave Kelly, but everyone was trying to save something and put it away.

My father had a two-story house and he and my step-mother were carrying everything upstairs. And they had a lit-tle boy they had raised. His mother had died in Kelly the night he was born and my folks raised him. He was 13 years old. They sent him over to the store to the phone, and he

In 1925 the Gros Ventre Slide dammed the river of the same name. Two years later the natu-ral dam burst, flooding the town of Kelly and killing six people. Jackson Hole Historical Society and Museum, BC.0274.

called me to come after them, but I couldn't get our model T Ford started. I went down in the field to get Andy to get it started and he said, "Oh, get dinner on the table, and we'll go over as soon as we have dinner." But the flood hit about noon, and so we never had a chance to get over to Kelly. My parents and that little boy, Joe Farley his name was, were all drowned in the flood and their bodies were found the next day—except my father's. It was two weeks before his body was found.

Local homesteader J. R. Jones actually saw the Kelly flood and wrote about it. These are some of his descriptions.

> The morning of May 18, 1927, was clear and warm. For about four days the snow had been melting rapidly and all streams had risen to considerable height. At about 10:30 the waters began rising at the estimated rate of one foot a minute and shortly afterward the bridge at Kelly went out.
>
> The crest of the flood as it burst upon the town was a terrifying sight, for it carried a twenty-five-feet high battering front of logs, trees, houses, and outbuildings. Every business house and residence was swept away and left not a trace of their former location. The church and school house, being on a higher elevation of land, escaped destruction.
>
> The battering wall [of the flood] hit the [Gros Ventre River highway] bridge half way from [the] floor to [the] top of [the] steel, and the great spans rose up and dropped into the current. . . . At times great logs leaped high in the air like barbed monsters of the seas.
>
> In less than an hour the waters commenced lowering where the highway bridge had stood on the Gros Ventre River. At 6:30 the next morning Birch Hopson forded on a saddle horse and was there when I reached the crossing.

The Kelly flood caused a great deal of damage and misery in its short time. But it left behind an unexpected gift for the Mormon Row homesteaders. Cliff Hansen described it in a speech at the Jackson Hole Historical Society and Museum:

> Prior to 1927, there was no open water in Mormon Row. Livestock were watered by pumping from wells. Ditch Creek regularly iced over and ceased flowing in the vicinity of the present location of the Teton Science School. The Kelly land slide of 1925, followed by the flood of 1927, changed things for those hard-working homesteaders. In 1927 a warm spring erupted a mile north of Kelly. The flood of 1927, caused by the partial failure of the dam, swept away the town of Kelly, but it created a warm water supply for the livestock which Mormon Row ranchers kept in increasing numbers. The grateful ranchers named it Miracle Spring.

The Chambers children went to the Grovont school until they started high school, which was in the town of Jackson. It was too far to commute, so the family had a choice to make. Their choice was simplified when their new home on Mormon Row suddenly burned to the ground. They bought a house in town.

Ida made their new home available to other Mormon Row children who were ready for high school. "My mother kept kids from all along the Row in town, so they could go to school," said Roy. "It had been traditional for people who lived out in the valley to send the kids to family in Rexburg to go to school. The kids got real homesick over there, so it was great to have them stay with Ida in town."

"There were so many children in that house that the noise often got overwhelming," Gladys May Kent remembers. "One day Ida was trying to work and finally Andy walked in and said, 'My God, how do you stand the noise?' Ida said, 'Well, I can't really stand it, but I don't know how to shut them up. If you can think of something, do.' So Andy took a nickel out of his pocket and he put it over the door and he said, 'The last person to talk gets this nickel.' You could have heard a pin drop in that house. I can't remember who got the nickel, but Reese Chambers talked first."

In November 1945, Andy Chambers suddenly died. He was fifty-six years old. At the age of forty-eight, Ida was a widow with seven children ages nine to twenty-five. Her older sons Roy and Reese continued to operate the ranch, and Ida joined them for a few years. Over the years, she and her children sold their ranch to what would become Grand Teton National Park, retaining a lifetime lease so that the ranch remained in the family into the 1980s.

When her daughter "Peach" was a junior at the University of Wyoming, she invited Ida to spend the year with her. Ida was spunky enough to accept this unconventional invitation, and it was one she

Ida Chambers—still full of zest in her later years, n.d. Photo by Olie Riniker. Jackson Hole Historical Society and Museum, 2002. 0008.003.

never regretted. The summer after that college year Peach died at the age of twenty-one.

Ida's zest for life remained unabated into her older years. With her trailer, she traveled as far as Mexico. She was a dedicated rockhound and spent most winters in Arizona. When she was eighty-two she married her longtime friend Henry Francis. They were well-suited for each other, sharing numerous interests and friends. When she was eighty-four, Ida was honored for her life in Jackson Hole. As she left their home to have her photograph taken for the occasion, her husband asked her where she was going. "I've got a date downtown, Henry," she replied. "I'll be back before fall!"

Henry died when Ida was eighty-seven, and still she kept her positive outlook. She was two months short of turning ninety-one when she died in 1988. Her family said of her, "Ida maintained her zest for life no matter what until the last few months of her life. She could find something good in almost everything that came her way." Ida is buried next to Andy in the Aspen Hill Cemetery in Jackson.

The Andy Chambers Ranch is listed in the National Register of Historic Places because it "represents Mormon settlement in the area and is an important example of homesteading." This historic importance did not prevent the ranch from being allowed to deteriorate— along with other venerable buildings on Mormon Row. Over the years, many of these buildings have succumbed to harsh weather and neglect. In the summer of 1995, the Moulton family took action and restored Thomas Alma Moulton's historic barn, photographs of which have graced thousands of items—everything from postcards and calendars to jigsaw puzzles and the Jackson State Bank credit card—besides being featured in the Hollywood movie *Spencer's Mountain*.

Rescue for the Chambers Ranch came in the fall of 1995 and in the nick of time, since it was unlikely that the historic Chambers homestead buildings would have survived another winter. The rescue was spearheaded by Andy and Ida's granddaughter, Judy Crandall.

Thanks to her determination, to a remarkable group called the Michigan Volunteers, to a change in attitude at Grand Teton National Park, and to help from local volunteers and businesses, Judy was successful. Together, this combination launched the rescue of Mormon Row and the stabilization of deteriorating buildings began. In the summer of 2003, the Michigan Volunteers completed their last remaining project on Mormon Row.

Who are these wonderful Michigan Volunteers? They are a small group of amateur carpenters, some of them with Habitat for Humanity experience. Under the leadership of Ed Brown, they made a commitment to preservation in Grand Teton National Park. Most of them are from Michigan, but one member comes all the way from England. They range in age from teenagers to a lively woman of eighty-eight who over the years has been capturing the team's activities in sketches and watercolors. The Michigan Volunteers pay their own expenses, sleep in tents, and work long hours. "Some of those buildings were literally on the ground," says Ed Brown, "and we were able to save them."

In 2002, the volunteers worked on Mormon Row and on the Geraldine Lucas homestead. Ed Brown recalls, "This was the first year where we were visited by officials from the park [including the new Superintendent] as well as the head of the National Trust for Historic Preservation, who said that our crew were his 'preservation heroes.' "

In October 2003, the National Trust for Historic Preservation presented the Michigan Volunteers and their Jackson Hole liason, Lorna Miller, with the prestigious National Preservation Honor Award for their work in Grand Teton National Park. "Without their work," said National Trust president Richard Moe, "many of the Park's historic structures and buildings on Mormon Row would be in ruins today." The Park plans to create a self-guided walking tour through Mormon Row for the public.

Fortunately for the remaining historic buildings in Grand Teton National Park, the Michigan Volunteers and Lorna Miller are continu-

Top: The Michigan Volunteers at work preserving the historic Andy Chambers homestead on Mormon Row in 1995. "Preserving" is the technical term for the stabilization work that was done on the old cabin. Photo by Mark Huffman. Courtesy *Jackson Hole News and Guide*. Bottom: The "Bunkhouse" at Moulton Ranch Cabins, now preserved, was originally a cabin on Thomas Alma Moulton's 1907 Mormon Row homestead, 2003. Photo courtesy of Brad Moulton.

ing their preservation work at other historic sites. Next on their agenda are the Geraldine Lucas homestead and the Bar BC Ranch.

Mormon Row has been part of Grand Teton National Park for many years. But one acre, right near the famous Moulton barn, is still owned by the Moulton family. It was a wedding present from Thomas Alma Moulton to his son Clark when he married Veda May, the granddaughter of James I. May. Clark and Veda Moulton made their home there for many years. The historic property, with its fabulous unspoiled view, is now owned by Clark and Veda's grandson and his wife. Staying in the restored Moulton homestead building at the well-kept Moulton Ranch Cabins is the closest modern visitors can come to experiencing the remarkable community that was Mormon Row.

CHAPTER SEVEN

GERALDINE LUCAS

ARRIVED IN JACKSON HOLE IN 1912

⊱⊶⊷⊙⊷⊶⊰

Geraldine Lucas homesteaded her land as a single woman. This fact places her historically in the small category of remarkable women who actually homesteaded on their own. She was also remarkable in that she lived an independent life decades before this was deemed socially acceptable for a woman. Geraldine did not explain herself to others, but her actions were writ large, and they speak volumes.

Her story begins in Iowa City, Iowa. She was born Geraldine Adorna Lucas on November 5, 1865, the sixth of Robert and Adeline Woods Lucas's eleven children. Her father's father had been Governor of Ohio, and in 1838 President Martin Van Buren appointed him the first territorial Governor of Iowa. Geraldine's father avoided his father's kind of public life and left Iowa City with his young family to homestead in eastern Nebraska. Like him, his daughter eventually chose to leave cities and public life and turned to open spaces and living on the land.

As her mother had, Geraldine went to college, and she chose the same college. Her mother enrolled at Oberlin College in Ohio in 1856. Oberlin was an educational pioneer. In 1833, it became the first college in the nation to open its doors to women as well as men. Famous women's colleges like Mount Holyoke, Vassar, Smith, Wellesley,

Radcliffe, and Bryn Mawr soon followed, but Oberlin was the first to champion women in this way. Adeline Woods dropped out of Oberlin after one year to marry Robert Lucas, but she taught and helped organize schools in Nebraska. From her, Geraldine gained an appreciation for learning and education that never left her.

When she was nineteen years old, Geraldine married Michael O'Shea, a thirty-year-old Kansas jeweler and optician. Less than two years later, and six months pregnant, she left him and returned to her family in Nebraska, where her son, Russell, was born. At age twenty-one, she was already living life on her own terms, crossing boundaries that few women in her time even came near. She left a marriage at a time when that step was not socially sanctioned for women. When divorced, she not only took back her family name but took the highly unusual step of insisting that her son's last name be legally changed to Lucas as well. Why? No one seems to know. Geraldine Lucas never spoke about her marriage. It remained a closed book.

Geraldine and her son stayed with her family for four years. Then came her next unconventional step. She moved to Ohio and enrolled in Oberlin College's preparatory department. Two years later, she entered Oberlin as a freshman. A single mother with her small son, she

Geraldine Lucas as she appeared in the Oberlin class of 1898 yearbook. Oberlin College Archives, Oberlin, Ohio.

successfully graduated in 1898 with a bachelor's degree. She was thirty-two years old, a "mature student" nearly a century before that term became commonplace. This is probably why she lied to Oberlin about her age, subtracting five years to seem closer to the age of other women students.

With her Oberlin degree, Geraldine went to New York City to teach. Here, she raised her son, whom she always called Razz, while teaching music, art, and sewing in the public school system. She worked very hard to educate her son, hoping that he would graduate from one of the Ivy League colleges. But Razz had other ideas. At the age of sixteen, he ran away from home and joined the Navy as a sailor on board a ship that was away from New York for more than two years. When he returned, Geraldine persuaded him to finish high school. He did so, but then bypassed the Ivy League to enter what is now the Coast Guard Academy. He made a career in the Coast Guard and at the time reportedly was the youngest man ever to be commissioned to the rank of commander. Unfortunately for his mother, as commander of the Coast Guard cutter *Baird*, he spent much of his time in remote Alaskan waters.

The year after Razz graduated from the Coast Guard Academy and clearly had a career he wanted, Geraldine retired from teaching in New York and headed for Jackson Hole, where two of her brothers and her sister had homesteaded and were ranching. She joined her Jackson Hole family in 1912 and immediately set out to buy thirty-eight acres along Phelps Lake near Jackson Hole's first dude ranch, the JY. She was able to buy this property through the Timber and Stone Act, a federal law by which people could buy public land that the government deemed unlikely to prove agriculturally productive. Certainly, her land was agriculturally unproductive; but, as the JY dude ranch would amply demonstrate, it was potentially very productive in the budding tourist trade.

In buying this property, on which she never lived, Geraldine followed a pattern of other single women homesteaders who acquired public land as an investment in order to sell it at a profit and thus earn money at a time when jobs for women were scarce and salaries minimal. She paid $3.25 an acre plus a $10 filing fee for this potentially choice property.

The place she picked to homestead and live on is considered one of the most beautiful sites in Jackson Hole. Her home sits at the base of the Teton Range, almost at the foot of the Grand Teton, in a flowering meadow dotted with stands of pine, cottonwood, and aspen trees. From her cabin she had a fine view of the Teton Range and, since she was known to rise at dawn, she could also see the first rays of the sun illuminate the 13,770 foot summit of the Grand Teton. A tribute written at her death says that Geraldine "never failed to get a thrill from the grandeur and magnificence of that great granite mass towering above her." That is easy to believe for anyone who has been to the site of her home, whatever the season.

When Geraldine Lucas filed on her homestead as a single woman, she joined the ten to twelve percent of all homesteaders who were women. But almost all of those women homesteaded as part of a family. A married woman could not file for a patent to expand her husband's homestead, but an unmarried woman in the family could. So unmarried sisters, daughters, fiancées, and mothers-in-law filed in order to improve their family assets. The women who homesteaded on their own, proved up, and got their patent were rare indeed. The popular literature written about these women made them the stuff of legend.

Geraldine was nearly forty-eight years old in the summer of 1913 when she moved onto her homestead and started the work of proving up. She hired a local log builder to build a two-room log cabin, working hard along with him. She plowed three acres and planted a garden. In the fall, she laid in supplies for her long winter in isolation. Firewood, of course, and other basics. But also enough loaves of bread to last her all winter. She would bring in one frozen loaf at a time from

Geraldine Lucas's log home below the Grand Teton, n.d. Jackson Hole Historical Society and Museum, 1958.1646.001.

storage and heat it in her oven, which made it taste almost like a fresh-ly baked loaf. She also bought about six dozen cakes of varieties she liked and, one after another throughout the winter, she put them through the same procedure. Those who knew her said she was a good cook, but she did not like to cook.

For this first long winter in her little log cabin, with outside tem-peratures down to 40 degrees below zero, she had only the most basic equipment: a wood stove for heating and cooking, a bed, a table, a few chairs, a kerosene lamp, and an outdoor privy. She carried water from nearby Cottonwood Creek when it wasn't frozen over; when it was, she had to melt snow. She was about five miles on snowshoes from her nearest neighbors and ten miles from the nearest stage line to Jackson. She chose this life with its long months of solitude, and she enjoyed it.

In the summers, she visited family and friends for weeks at a time. Once winter set in, she settled down with her piano, her sewing machine and her many books—at her death she had a library of more than 1,350 books, all carefully cataloged. She was an expert seamstress and "would sew until hell wouldn't have it," according to her nephew. He never knew what she did with all the clothes she made, since she her-self always wore knickers. She fashioned them from cut-off jeans and wore them with black stockings and a variety of blouses and jackets. Her nephew said he *never* saw her in a dress. This was at a time when most women wore dresses even when they worked in the field—and some, not so long before, wore corsets under their dresses in the field.

The following year Geraldine plowed 20 acres and planted wheat, but hail pummeled the entire crop and destroyed it. For the next six years she seeded 20 acres with timothy, a grass used for fodder. She built a log house for her son Razz and his family, a log storehouse, a granary, a rabbit house, a fence, and two ditches, which together added up to two and a half miles. She valued these improvements at $7,000. No one knows the details of her finances. She called herself a rancher, but she lived in her home for twenty-four years until her death with no

Top: Geraldine Lucas's cabin in winter, n.d. The cabin she built for her son is behind hers, and farther back is Naomi Colwell's cabin. Jackson Hole Historical Society and Museum, 1958.1752.001.

Left: Geraldine Lucas in her customary garb, n.d. Photo by Harrison Crandall. Courtesy of the Crandall family.

apparent income from her homestead. Possibly, she had some retire-
ment income. Probably, her son sent her money. He appears to have
been caring and generous toward his mother, whom he visited regularly before he married. After he married, he brought his wife and moth-
er-in-law with him to visit. He certainly provided his mother with an
Alaskan sled and dog team, complete with Alaskan boots and parka.
This gift made it a great deal easier for his mother to enjoy some winter social life with her friends and neighbors at Jenny Lake.

Geraldine Lucas was called a loner. She was also called a hermit.
These terms described the way people often saw how she had chosen to
live her life. They did not describe the way Geraldine, herself, saw her
life. She always said that she never felt lonely, that living by herself suited her. So it seems surprising that, after a few years, she invited a young
woman she had just met to homestead right next to her home.

The young woman was twenty-three-year-old Naomi Colwell,
daughter of a well-to-do Michigan family. In 1918, the family went
across country to California. On their way through Jackson Hole they
stopped to visit Geraldine Lucas. Why they did so is not known. When
her family went on to California, Naomi stayed behind and proceeded
to take up a homestead next to Geraldine's.

There is little doubt that this was done in alliance with Geraldine,
who clearly helped Naomi apply for the 160-acre homestead, prove up
as required, and get her final patent. Naomi's property already had a
cabin on it, but she built a new cabin in 1919. They shared ranch work.
They often shared meals, apparently in Naomi's cabin. And they were
known to go together in Geraldine's dogsled for winter trips to the post
office and to visit neighbors. Naomi seeded ten acres with timothy; the
following year, she seeded twenty-six acres with winter wheat. Other
improvements in her proving up included a log barn, fencing, and a
quarter-mile ditch.

Naomi was a city girl from Michigan, so it is reasonable to con-
clude that she could not have homesteaded and proved up without

Top: Christmas Party, 1925. Geraldine Lucas joins her friends near Jenny Lake for the festivi-ties. Left to right: Leonard Timmermeyer, Lida Gabbey, Hildegard and Harrison Crandall, Tony Grace, Geraldine Lucas, and Albert Gabbey. Courtesy of the Crandall family. Bottom: Geraldine Lucas with her son Russell, his wife, Alice, and her mother, n.d. Jackson Hole Historical Society and Museum, 1991.3780.001.

major support from Geraldine, who knew homesteading work from her childhood and from her own proving up in Jackson Hole. In the spring of 1922, Naomi completed her required three-year homestead residency and had proved up her property. The Interior Department then issued Naomi Colwell a final patent for her homestead. Geraldine Lucas and her brother Lee Lucas served as witnesses for Naomi to receive her papers.

Less than two months later, Naomi sold her homestead to Geraldine for $500 and a return ticket to Michigan. When she arrived back home from the West, Naomi wore full western cowgirl gear, complete with boots and a ten-gallon hat. Her friends greeted her as a heroine.

Why would these two very different women, an elderly recluse and a young city woman, get together the way they did? The deal they "cooked up," as Geraldine's nephew phrased it, probably explains the mystery. Since both women agreed to the deal and stuck to it, it probably suited them.

Naomi Colwell's cabin, 2004. It was built in 1919 and preserved between 2003 and 2005. Photo by Charles Craighead. Jackson Hole Historical Society and Museum, 2005.0125.001.

What was in the deal for Geraldine? Probably this: it was a way to acquire more land, something most western homesteaders tried to do because the standard 160-acre homestead was not enough land for ranching in the West. It could also have been a way for her to acquire land as an investment for future profit, something many single women homesteaders did, and what Geraldine herself probably did when she bought her 38 acres on Phelps Lake. Homestead law did not allow her to homestead another 160 acres. But through this deal with Naomi, and without breaking any law, Geraldine could simply buy the land she wanted.

For Naomi, this deal was a way for a city girl to have a genuine western adventure, with all that such an adventure implied. And at this particular time, it implied a great deal to thousands of urban women. For nearly a decade, urban women had avidly been reading about single women homesteaders in the West. This popular literature was published widely in both magazines and books. Its theme spoke strongly to women at a time when the women's suffrage movement had gained strength, and many women were seeking to redefine their lives in more individualistic terms. The popular stories about the adventures of single women homesteaders created a western version of New Womanhood, with images of independent women who successfully staked a claim. They emphasized risk-taking in an unfamiliar world, where women pushed their own limits and emerged with a broader sense of their own capabilities.

Geraldine's invitation to Naomi that she become a single woman homesteader fit right into the "I did it!" image promoted by this popular literature. Naomi actually became a single woman homesteader. She "did it!" She succeeded in the great adventure promised by the popular literature. Having done so, she returned in glory to her city, dressed in full western cowgirl regalia and was treated as a heroine.

In striking their deal, then, each woman was responding in her own way to specific historic conditions of her time. Each woman had her reasons, and each woman got what she wanted out of their arrangement. The temporary union probably had its rough times, given the great differences between the two, but it worked for both of them. When Geraldine and Naomi completed the deal and gained their desired benefits, each woman returned to her own way of life.

Are there any people still living who knew Geraldine Lucas? A few, and this is how two of them describe her. "They said if you can work for Mrs. Lucas, you can work for anybody," said Bob Kranenberg, who often worked for her. One time he had just stacked her firewood when she appeared. "How come the bark isn't up on that piece of wood there?" she immediately inquired. "The piece was about three or four tiers down," Bob explained. "I had to tear that pile down and do it over. She was really something else to work with."

Another time, Bob was housecleaning with Geraldine when a man showed up, uninvited. Geraldine was notorious for discouraging uninvited arrivals and was true to form. "She barked at the man, 'What are you doing here? You know I'm house-cleaning.' 'Could I use your privy?' the man said. 'No,' she says. 'We just scrubbed it and it isn't dry yet. You can go right behind that tree over there.' That's the type of person she was." Did Bob like her? "Oh, yes," he said. "She was a very unusual person. The first meeting or two you'd think, she's really blunt, there's no messing around with her. You'd know how she felt about something. She'd tell you. She didn't hesitate to say if she didn't like something. But she was a very sincere person, and she tried to help people. I never once heard her talk against anybody."

Quita Pownall, the daughter of Geraldine's nearest neighbors, Harrison and Hildegard Crandall, knew Geraldine as a child. She remembers her as part of winter social times near Jenny Lake, with neighbors traveling back and forth across the snow to visit each other. "And Mother, who was a friend of Geraldine's, would see her through the summer. We were taken to her house to visit, and she came to our homestead to visit us. She had beautiful white hair. She was friendly to my sister and me. She paid attention when we showed her something, and she went huckleberrying with us. Her visits were always very nice. She was gracious and easy-going; and well-educated, which made her interesting. And she had *lots* of courage. You could just see that."

This courage was certainly evident in the summer of 1924, when Geraldine decided to climb the Grand Teton. She was nearly fifty-nine years old. Legendary mountaineer Paul Petzoldt was just sixteen years old at the time, and he had created a stir in the valley by announcing that he and a friend of his were going to climb the Grand Teton. The climbing expeditions started and ended near Geraldine's home, and William Owen (of the famous 1898 Grand Teton climb) brought Petzoldt and his friend out to meet her. In his memoir, *Teton Tales*, Petzoldt recounts what happened.

Harrison Crandall took this photograph of his friend Geraldine visiting with his two daughters, Quita and Nancy, c. 1933. Photo by Harrison Crandall. Courtesy of the Crandall family.

Mr. Owen said, "Geraldine is very choosy about her friends. She lives up there alone in this beautiful log house winter and summer. She doesn't like dudes to come visit her unless they're specifically invited." Soon we reached Cottonwood Creek . . . on the other side was Geraldine Lucas's house. She came out looking quite stern until she recognized Mr. Owen. "What are you people up to now?" she asked. "These boys are going to climb the Grand Teton, or think they are at least," Mr. Owen said. "Perhaps when they come down or if they have any trouble they could stop here on their way back."

"You're going to climb the Grand Teton?" she asked. "Well, we're sure going to try," I said. "I've dreamed of doing that myself." she said. "Maybe if you get up there, I can make it too." She assured us that we would be welcome on our return trip.

Paul Petzoldt, age sixteen. He had just made a notable ascent of the Grand Teton and would soon guide Geraldine Lucas to the summit, 1924. Jackson Hole Historical Society and Museum, 2003. 0050.052.

Petzoldt and his friend successfully climbed the Grand Teton, but Geraldine was not at home when they got down.

Soon after their climb, Geraldine went to see Petzoldt. "She asked me point blank if I would take her to the top of the Grand Teton. 'I've heard talk around town that it's no place for a woman and that women should not be allowed up there,' she said. 'People just don't understand women like myself.' I had been warned by some of the locals that Geraldine was difficult to get along with and hard to understand, but I found her friendly and her great intelligence stimulating. She had seen the Grand Teton in all its moods and had long had a great desire to reach its summit. In many conversations, I encouraged her and empathized with her ambition. I was determined to help her get to the top of the mountain she loved."

And help her he did. In his book, he describes a memorable climb and reveals aspects of Geraldine Lucas's character that no one else appears to have seen or appreciated the way he did. On the climb, he took the lead and put her directly behind himself, so she could follow in his footsteps and imitate his climbing style. Four men from Kelly met them on the mountain. They were carrying an American flag on a pole, so that friends down in Kelly could see it waving in the wind from the top of the Grand and prove that they had been up there. Two of the men decided the climb was too much. The other two joined Petzoldt's party, carrying the flag. They all made it past the notorious Belly Roll and narrow Crawl with its 3,000 foot sheer drop and were nearly there. This is Petzoldt's description of Geraldine's arrival at the summit of the Grand Teton.

> I kept Geraldine on the rope and she followed directly behind me. When we got a few feet from the top I stopped, took ahold of Geraldine's hand, and brought her around to the front. I patted her on the back and urged her to the summit first. She was silent as she looked down at her cabin, a speck way below. As I came up, she grabbed me and hugged

me. I thought perhaps I heard soft crying. But as the others arrived, Geraldine regained her composure. I don't think she often broke through her protected personality, but in that moment when she threw her arms around me with a soft sob, I sensed the real Geraldine Lucas, an intelligent, loving woman who had elected for some reason to leave most of society behind.

Then the rounds of picture taking started. It was a patriotic moment and I will remember forever one shot of Geraldine standing on top, her arms outspread, with the flag flying behind her.

After her momentous climb of the Grand Teton, Geraldine settled back into daily life on her beloved property. A letter she wrote to an Oberlin classmate, with photographs, gives the flavor of her feelings. "Pictures are very unsatisfactory to convey the grandeur of the scenery. If you would like a real treat in that line tumble into your car about the last week in June or first in July and ramble out to the Teton National Park in the Jackson Hole Country and view the scenery for yourself. The very best in the United States and for that matter anywhere else. And, Oh Joy! I have a corner to the most majestic of it all."

Geraldine Lucas was no fan of the federal government and the General Land Office, and certainly her frustrations with that office's handling of her homesteading claim would not inspire a positive attitude. In this, she joined many homesteaders who saw the General Land Office more as a hindrance than a help in their land dealings. Between 1927 and 1930, John D. Rockefeller, Jr., through the Snake River Land Company, purchased more than twenty-five thousand acres of Jackson Hole with the intention that the lands be donated to the National Park Service for a national park. Many people in the valley were happy to sell. Geraldine was not one of them. She was one of the "tough nuts" who refused to sell to Rockefeller's company. She was widely reported

August 19, 1924. Geraldine Lucas, soon to be sixty years old, stands on the summit of the Grand Teton. She was the first Jackson Hole woman to reach the summit and the second known woman ever to do so. Jackson Hole Historical Society and Museum, 1958.0351.001.

to have told a company agent, "You stack up those silver dollars as high as the Grand Teton and I might talk to you." By 1932 company officials concluded that she would never sell.

But Horace Albright, one of the chief proponents of a national park in Jackson Hole, was not worried. He told Rockefeller, "She came out from the east and homesteaded under the Tetons because she wanted to spend the rest of her life within sight of these mountains. She is a lover of beauty and nature, and I am very certain that she would not allow her property to be put to any objectionable commercial uses."

And she never did. When she was nearing seventy, she began to think of the best future for her beloved home. She wrote to an Oberlin College friend, "I wonder if Oberlin College would care to establish a summer school among this beautiful scenery. You might find out for me. I don't expect to live forever, growing old and unattractive, but still retain a deep love for Oberlin College."

Before she settled the future of her home, Geraldine died. In the summer of 1938, she became ill while visiting friends and was taken to the Jackson hospital. Her son was notified and started to drive to Jackson Hole with his wife and daughter. His mother died of heart failure one hour before they reached the hospital. At Geraldine's request, the urn with her ashes was placed in a hollow that was chiseled out of a large rock in a meadow near her home. A bronze plaque over the hollow says, "Geraldine A. Lucas, 1865–1938."

Since Geraldine died without a will, her son inherited all her property. A year after her death, he sold her land to J. D. Kimmel, who also owned the Jenny Lake store and post office, a gasoline service station, and a large cabin area for tourists along the highway.

Kimmel intended to divide Geraldine's homestead into lots and sell them to people for homes or vacation cabins, a plan Geraldine would have detested possibly even more than having her land go to the National Park Service. This is when a four-year-old girl came to play a pivotal role in changing Kimmel's plan.

Kimmel already had a number of his Lucas lots spoken for when he met Harold Fabian, who was Rockefeller's chief agent for buying land in Jackson Hole. Up to then, Kimmel had had no intention of selling to Rockefeller. Enter Toli Sombrero, a four-year-old Indian girl who was visiting the park superintendent's wife for the summer. In her history, *The Lucas Place: 1914–1975*, Mrs. Josephine Fabian wrote that Kimmel "had a great case on the little girl, and she really was the connecting link between Mr. Kimmel and Mr. Fabian becoming good friends." The little girl called Kimmel "Uncle Kimmel," which is how he became known in the valley.

Kimmel took a great liking to Harold Fabian and changed his mind about selling his Lucas property. In a conversation that has been widely quoted in the valley, he said, "Fabian, I can ruin your whole damn project." Knowing that Kimmel's large property lay in the heart of the proposed national park, Fabian replied, "I know you can, Uncle Kimmel." Kimmel paused for a few suspenseful moments and then said, "But I ain't a goin' to. Tell you what I'm willin' to do. I'll sell you the Lucas Place for just what I paid for it. And I'll also sell you the whole Jenny Lake outfit—the store, the cabins, the gasoline station, the whole shootin' match—for just what I paid for all of them. Provided you'll give Lura and me a lease back on the cabins, store layout and my cabins across the creek, for as long as either of us live."

Kimmel and Fabian struck a deal then and there. And so, in time, Geraldine Lucas's property did become part of Grand Teton National Park. And the big cabin she built for her son and his family became Harold Fabian's Jackson Hole headquarters and summer home for the rest of his life.

Geraldine Lucas's home and other buildings, as well as Naomi Colwell's cabin, are now officially listed on the National Register of Historic Places. The listing states: " . . . The Geraldine Lucas Homestead is unusual as the home of a pioneering single woman. In subsequent years, the cabin served as the summer home of Harold Fabian, who spearheaded John D. Rockefeller's successful effort to expand the boundaries of Grand Teton National Park to include the valley floor. . . . The district's period of significance extends from 1913, when Geraldine Lucas first filed for patent to 160 acres, until 1950 when Congress extended Grant Teton National Park." The homestead is important, too, as a fine example of Rustic architecture.

Geraldine Lucas lived an independent, solitary life that crossed many boundaries of acceptable behavior for women in her time. The unconventional aspects of her behavior, which in her time made her susceptible to charges of eccentricity, and worse, are now—as historian Sherry Smith has noted—choices that western women can make with far fewer costs. Perhaps sixteen-year-old Paul Petzoldt, standing on top of the Grand Teton with Geraldine, most accurately described the woman whose character eluded many twice his age: Geraldine Lucas was a bright, loving soul who, for unknown reasons, elected to leave society behind.

CHAPTER EIGHT

THE DORNAN FAMILY

ARRIVED IN JACKSON HOLE IN 1922

━┅◆┅○┅◆┅━

Dornan's in Moose is a Jackson Hole landmark. This family enterprise is now run by the third generation of Dornans. And it all started because a Philadelphia socialite divorcee wanted a change.

She was Evelyn Middleton Dornan, daughter of a wealthy industrialist, and was born into Philadelphia mainline society in 1881. The Middletons were a prominent Quaker family who could trace their roots back to Arthur Middleton, who signed the Declaration of Independence. Evelyn's father died while he was still in his fifties, and he left an interesting will. "The way I heard the story," Evelyn's grandson Bob Dornan recalls, "he set up trust funds for his kids. If his wife remarried within two years of his death, she would get nothing from the estate. Well, his wife remarried about a year after his death, so his entire fortune was divided among the kids." Evelyn's inheritance made her independently wealthy and able to live life entirely as she pleased. She proceeded to do just that.

Her first step was fairly conventional in terms of her background. When she was twenty-one, she married John P. Dornan, who also came from an old Quaker family with roots going back to the

Revolution. The family business, Dornan's Carpet and Rugs Co., Inc., had earned a lot of money making saddle blankets during the Civil War, and John Dornan had the reputation of being a playboy. He did become a lawyer. But his real passion was sports, and he was a famous cricket player with the Philadelphia Cricket Club.

Their son, John P. Dornan, Jr., who was called Jack, would create Dornan's in Moose. He was born in 1904. While Jack was growing up, his father worked for the DuPont family. This meant that the Dornan family lived at Montpelier in Virginia, the luxurious DuPont estate that had once belonged to James Madison, the fourth President of the United States. A family photo of Jack at about age eleven shows him on the estate with his own horse and cart.

"From time to time my father would tell stories about his childhood," says Dave Dornan. "Certainly, his childhood had many privileges that were amazing, such as being able to live at the DuPont estate

Opposite page: Dornan's in Moose as it looked in the 1950s after Jack Dornan had built his Chuckwagon Restaurant, complete with tipis. Courtesy of the Dornan family.

Right Jack Dornan as a young boy, c. 1915. Courtesy of the Dornan family.

in Virginia. But he was also a neglected and unwanted child who spent much of his youth growing up either at summer camps or at boarding schools. He came to Jackson Hole knowing nothing about the practical world and had to become self-sufficient."

Jack Dornan's coming to Jackson Hole took a circuitous route that reflected his parents' divorce and his mother's choices for her own life. John and Evelyn Dornan divorced while Jack was attending St. James Preparatory Academy in Virginia. He stayed there while his father began to fade out of his life, and his mother focused exclusively on her own desires.

It was late 1917, and the U.S. had entered World War I. "I felt the urge to do War work," Evelyn wrote in her diary. By the following spring, she had passed the Civil Service and medical examinations. "March 8th, 1918, I entered the YMCA Aircraft School, paying $30 for a 4 weeks course. The day after I finished I entered the Naval Aircraft Factory."

Her workday at the factory was from 7:30 a.m. to 6 p.m., with a half hour for lunch. "I got $11.04 for my first week and $15.33 for my second. I have bought 2 Liberty Bonds, one while in training and the second after hearing a wonderful sailor at the lunch hour."

She and her women co-workers made wings for airplanes. "We finished the first women's wing on Friday at noon. It took us just a week . . . The Chief Inspector said, 'I have to hand it to you—it's a fine wing.' Stanley, our leading man, is tickled to death—he says it's a better wing than the men make and we called upon him less than men do."

That summer, she got her first furlough and decided to visit a distant relative who had settled in Moose. "Thursday, July 18, 1918. Bought my return ticket as far as Pocatello. I leave on Wednesday, July 24th for my visit to Maud Noble, Jackson Hole, Wyo. $128.35." She took sixteen-year-old Jack with her on this trip, but she rarely mentions him in her diary.

Top: Evelyn Dornan in Jackson Hole, probably with Jimmy Manges, in 1919. Courtesy of the Dornan family.

Left: Evelyn Dornan in Philadelphia, c. 1918, probably about the time she decided to come west. Courtesy of the Dornan family.

Her diary suggests that she was coming to Jackson Hole looking for adventure and for someone to confide in after her divorce. She found both: "Wednesday, July 30th. This morning I had my first horse-back lesson. Dewey Van Winkle, a *real* cow-boy gave me a lesson on his horse. He rode one and led mine. He says I will learn all right. I had a good talk with Maud right off. She understands."

And less than two weeks later in her diary: "I am surely having the time of my life. The country is magnificent. The Teton mountains tower right over us. Last night we did not get home until after dark, almost 10 o'clock I should say. We have ridden to Jenny's Lake, Timber Island, the Bar BC Ranch."

That fall, she went back East to build airplane wings for the war, and Jack went back to his prep school. She returned with him the next summer and rented the loft of Jimmy Manges's picturesque barn, which still stands near the Taggart Lake trailhead. Her diary shows her going on major horseback pack trips into Death Canyon, writing detailed notes about valley flora and fauna, making friends with the homesteaders in the Moose area. And then: "Bought Peggy and her colt Kamal." She was beginning to settle in.

By the summer of 1922, when Moose homesteader Holiday Menor showed Evelyn some vacant land adjoining his homestead, she filed for it right away. Her diary says, simply, "Got my homestead August 21st. 20 59/100 acres south of Holiday's." Historically, she was one of the first single woman homesteaders in Jackson Hole. Personally, she was a woman who took on the Homestead Act bureaucracy and was going to bend it to her will. In this she succeeded 100 percent. As her grandson Dave said of her, "Gran was a strong, determined independent woman who knew what she wanted and got it."

Evelyn named her 20-plus acres Spur Ranch, for the World War I British cavalry spurs that a favorite English friend had given her. The spurs are still in the family, and a photograph of them hangs in Dornan's bar. Spur Ranch was a small property, far too small for regular homesteading in Jackson Hole, where even 160 acres was barely sufficient for a family to survive. But at that point, Evelyn was not looking to settle and survive. She wanted to have a summer house in Jackson Hole, and for this purpose the property sufficed admirably. Surrounded by two major homesteads, it sat snugly beside the Snake River, and it had one of the most stupendous views in the entire valley.

Evelyn Dornan's home as it grew in Moose, n.d. Jackson Hole Historical Society and Museum, 2005.0045.016.

Evelyn's property had previously been used by a man who had a blacksmith practice there. His business went broke and he abandoned the place, leaving behind a log building with a sod roof, dirt floor, and one side open where the smithy had been. "There were no windows in the darn thing," laughs grandson Bob Dornan. "Gran got a couple of local carpenters to put on a new roof. They boarded up the open wall and made a doorway; they put in a floor and cut some windows in the log walls. That was the original cabin. Over the years she added onto it, a room here, another there. It was sort of a ramshackle building, but it served her purposes very well."

Evelyn's diary for September, 1922, has several entries about things she added to her Spur Ranch house—minimal household furnishings to make do with until she and Jack left for the winter. Her diary never mentions the really big event: Jack had decided to stay in Jackson Hole. He refused to return to St. James Preparatory Academy and his waiting appointment to West Point. Unwelcome as his decision was to his mother, he stuck to it. If he had not, there probably never would have been a Dornan's in Moose.

It must have been quite a confrontation. According to Bob, it was. Gran "was rather a spoiled woman and very prejudiced in her ideas . . . She had her way of doing things, and it was right, and to hell with everybody else . . . Dad told me this story years and years later." She finally told him, "All right, stay then. I'm leaving." She gave him fifty dollars and said, "Go buy some groceries to get you through the winter." And then she took off for California.

So there was teenage Jack, headed for a subzero winter in an unfinished cabin and totally unprepared to be self-sufficient. As he told Bob, "I didn't even know how to boil water. I spent about two weeks down in that cabin trying to get ready for winter. I didn't know what to do. But Holiday Menor up the river, he was keeping an eye on me. He knew Mrs. Evelyn Dornan and the situation. After she was gone for a couple of weeks, he came and knocked on the door. Old Holiday

Moose homesteader Holiday Menor, who offered teenager Jack Dornan a job at a crucial time, n.d. Jackson Hole Historical Society and Museum, 1958.0132.001.

knew how to read people. I was a smart ass kid and thought I knew everything, and Holiday knew that. He said to me, " 'Jack, why don't you come up and work for me this winter. I'm short-handed and I need some help.' Oh, God, I just grabbed at that. I worked up at Holiday's all winter. I learned how to feed cows, how to harness a team, how to do everything you do around a ranch. Boy, Holiday worked my tail off. I learned a lot. That spring, Holiday gave me fifty bucks."

This privileged dude boy from the East, as he was often labeled, learned to master the ways of Jackson Hole with remarkable effectiveness. During the summers he worked on Tony Grace's ranch, now Jenny Lake Lodge. His job helping to build the first trails up Death Canyon earned him the moniker "Death Canyon Jack." He learned the carpentry trade and log cabin building, becoming a skilled craftsman and building many of the log cabins at several dude ranches in the valley. He taught himself the electrical and plumbing trades. He also learned to hunt, fish, trap, ski, snowshoe, and bake potato bread. He was an unlikely but definite success. He loved Jackson Hole, and he stayed.

By 1925 it was time for Evelyn Dornan to convince the homestead authorities that she had proved up her homestead according to the rules, in order to get a patent to her land. The requirements included a three-year residence on the property, something her summer visits could never satisfy. She solved this problem by bringing Jack center stage. Every time she had to explain her absences, she wrote on the legal form, "My son remaining on ranch during my absence." And so he did. Jack's decision to stay on in Jackson Hole, which initially had infuriated his mother, now saved her. She got her final proof papers.

As it turned out, however, there was still trouble ahead. Evelyn's small acreage attracted the attention of Homestead Act land inspectors. It was clear that no one could viably homestead on 20 acres in Jackson Hole, so what was she doing with that property? The General Land Office sent Inspector C. S. Dietz to find out. Judging by his astonishing official report, Evelyn must have dazzled him with her high-society background and her widow status. She claimed to be "a widow with a minor son." To Mr. Dietz, this was likely a poignant and even noble condition. It was also pure fiction. Her supposedly dead husband had married again in 1922, and he and his wife already had the first of their two children. As for Jack, he was then twenty-two years old and hardly a minor.

"Death Canyon Jack" on horseback, c. 1920. Courtesy of the Dornan family.

Evelyn's strategy with Mr. Dietz was brilliant, and it worked. "Entrywoman emplaced her filing in the most scenic section of the State," he wrote in his report. (A full Teton view photograph was enclosed by him.) "Instead of defiling the entered scenic land by grazing domestic stock thereon, claimant has taken particular pains to see that only wild faunal life has direct access thereto." (Here a photograph of a visiting moose was enclosed.) "Claimant is a graduate of the Philadelphia Art Institute. In reality, her homestead entry is merely the final research laboratory or studio for the expression of her innate aesthetic abilities . . . In conducting the examination entrywoman was asked why she included but 20 acres in her entire homestead filing. She replied by saying that to connaturalize and beautify even a tract of that small dimension in a befitting manner, all of her spare time would be fully occupied. Thereupon it was concluded that if all clients of the Land Office were imbued with the extreme modesty and infinite sincerity of the entrywoman, the problem of administering the public domain would indeed become a considerably simplified procedure." Evelyn got her land patent.

Within a year, she was planning a subdivision on her homestead. The new road from Jackson to Moose included a steel truss bridge across the Snake River and went right by Spur Ranch. Evelyn got Jack to build three log cabins for rental. "It was the start of the first commercial idea for this property," says Bob. "And, you know, it didn't work out."

Jack's journey to a commercial idea that did work out would be long and tumultuous. Most happily for this young man with a self-centered mother and absent father, he had found someone with whom to share that journey. He had been courting her for years, and she finally consented. They were the first local couple to be married in the Chapel of the Transfiguration in Moose. Jack's bride was Ellen Jones, daughter of J. R. Jones and his wife Fidelia. Ellen had grown up in a close-knit family and in circumstances totally unlike Jack's. Where he came from old, tradition-bound Eastern high society, she came from a background that was the stuff of authentic western legend. Ellen's father was one of the most colorful men in Jackson Hole. And he was important to its future.

Joseph Reuben Jones was born in 1873 in the mining town of Gouge Eye near the town of You Bet, California, and grew up among a variety of gamblers. He quit school after the sixth grade to support himself as a "square" professional gambler (they did not cheat). His game was poker. For ten years, J. R. traveled the gold camps in Arizona and California. Then, in 1907, he came to Jackson Hole with his family to try a different kind of gambling—homesteading.

In "The Bet I Made With Uncle Sam," one of his many stories published in the popular press, he pinpointed the essence of homesteading in Jackson Hole: "The local land commissioner dropped the money into the drawer of his desk and handed me my receipt. As I stood a moment folding the precious paper the commissioner turned toward me and whimsically asked, 'Who wins?' 'What do you mean?' I inquired, puzzled. 'Why haven't you just bet Uncle Sam sixteen dollars against 160 acres of land that you can stick there for five years and not starve to death?' Naturally, I laughed, for it appealed to me as quite a joke . . . Yet grim reality eventually dulled the point of that joke for me."

J. R. Jones lost his bet with Uncle Sam, as did a number of other Jackson Hole homesteaders. He moved his family to Jackson, where he became a successful businessman and was elected to the first Town Council and to the Board of Education. He also became the valley's first outspoken supporter of Grand Teton National Park, even before his friend Struthers Burt, whom he joined at the famous meeting in Maud Noble's cabin in 1923. His writings and life story are collected in the book, *Preserving the Game: Gambling, Mining, Hunting, and Conservation in the Vanishing West*, published by the Hemingway Western Studies Center.

Joe and Fidelia Jones had six children, and Ellen was the second. She was born in 1903 in Sumpter, Oregon, and was four years old when her family moved to Jackson Hole. Joe and Fidelia spent considerable time teaching their children reading, writing, and arithmetic. Ellen's older brother Rodney, who became a physician, said of their parents, "Education was extremely important to them since they had both been deprived of any more than a limited education in their youth." They sought out the best educational opportunities for their children, even when it meant having them leave home.

"We Jones girls were educated at Ivison Hall [a Laramie boarding school], then at the University of Wyoming, where I gained a teaching certificate," Ellen told the Jackson Hole Historical Society and Museum. She was among the first women enrolled at the University of Wyoming.

When I returned to the valley, I taught at the Teton School over on Poker Flats, in the area now known as Teton Village. I boarded with the Flemings. They gave me a horse to ride to school. I had a first grader, second and third, which I could combine. There were only eight pupils in the little log school building at that time.

On week-ends, when weather permitted, I rode up to the STS dude ranch at Moose [presently the Murie Ranch] to visit my friends, Buster and Frances Estes. It would be dark by the time I arrived. Frances Estes and I were doing the cooking, cleaning, waiting tables, and entertaining the dudes at their place. I usually stayed over Saturday and rode back on Sunday.

Mrs. Estes was a debutante from Philadelphia who had come out west as a dude and married a cowboy. We became dear friends and she, in fact, became my Godmother. In the fall of 1926 I went east with the Estes. Frances was visiting her family back there. I taught at a private school in Amherst, Massachusetts, part of that winter.

It was through Frances and Buster Estes that Ellen met Jack Dornan, who, as she said, "was to occupy most of the rest of my life." They were married on October 11, 1927. Together, they would build the Dornan family business and raise seven children.

But in 1927, Dornan's in Moose was still a long way off. Jack took whatever odd jobs he could find through that winter. The newlyweds worked hard and had few diversions and very little money. Then Jack's mother stepped in, and his roller-coaster ride toward financial success took its first turn up.

Evelyn Dornan had been wintering in Southern California for some time, and she got Jack a job with a Lincoln dealer in La Jolla. "He had a great personality for talking to people," says his son Bob. "He

Jack and Ellen Dornan pose for their wedding photograph in the Chapel of Transfiguration, October 11, 1927. The Dornans were the first couple married in the Chapel. Courtesy of the Dornan family.

turned into the number one salesman in this Lincoln agency." He had just been offered the big job of running the agency's dealership for the whole state of Arizona when the stock market crash of 1929 hit, and he was out of a job.

Jack and Ellen returned to Jackson Hole. To make matters more precarious, they now had their first baby, Bob. Once again, Jack did anything he could to earn some money. This included working on John Wayne's first major movie, *The Big Trail (1930)*, whose most spectacular scenes were filmed in Jackson Hole. For a time, he ran his own business, Jackson Hole Freight Lines, between Salt Lake City and Jackson. It was the first of its kind and a good idea; all the same, it went broke in the aftermath of the 1929 crash.

In 1934, Jack began to establish a dude ranch at Spur Ranch. He built all the guest cabins, a snack bar, and a grocery store with a beer parlor upstairs—since Prohibition had ended in 1933. He put in a Texaco gas station. He also had a string of horses for the dudes to ride, and a prize herd of Jersey cows whose rich milk he sold to special places in the valley. Ellen worked right along with him—and sometimes alone. When Jack took people on hunting trips in the fall, she took care of the children, the ranch, and the dudes. This was the start of the now flourishing Dornan's in Moose.

The economy picked up by the late 1930s, and Jack added more log cabins to the property. Then he went to see his mother. He pointed out that he had made all the improvements on the property and that, if she wanted him to go ahead with the business, she would have to deed half the 20 acres to him for that purpose. "It was a fight," says Bob. "She had an even worse temper than Dad. But he was a real scrapper, and he won out. She deeded him the north half of the property in 1941. That's when he really started to build up the business."

The growing family prospered, but the winter isolation in Moose was still hard to take. "My God," Bob exclaims as he thinks back, "Wilson might as well have been ten thousand miles away. You heard the name Wilson, but you never got there. Moran was the same way. I remember a couple of winters when we actually got to Jackson one time, and that was on a sleigh."

But winter life in Moose also had its good times. "Dad was a great reader. He'd read books to us kids. You had to get your chores done first, then he'd read to us for an hour by a coal oil lamp, because we didn't have any electricity in those days. He'd read Kipling stories, *Winnie the Pooh* books and all those old kids' stories, and it would be great. He'd go so far, and then he'd say, 'That's all for today. Another day we'll continue on with this.' "

With better economic times came a radio—a battery-operated radio, since they still had no electricity. "We kids could pick some radio program. There were kids' programs like *The Green Hornet* and *Little Orphan Annie*. Monday nights, the *Lux Radio Theater* came on, and that was quiet

Bob Dornan, age seven, enjoys himself on skis, c. 1935. Courtesy of the Dornan family.

time, because that was the time Mother got to listen to the radio. Nobody made a sound while the *Lux Radio Theater* was on. That was her time. And, boy, if you got out of line and made noise, you heard about it."

Life was less peaceful in Grandmother's company. Bob recalls, "Every once in awhile in the summer, I'd go with Gran to Jackson for shopping. I remember one time we went into Mercill's dry goods store, where Harry the butcher had his shop. Harry didn't do exactly what she asked, and she blew up. She really cussed him out, and then she turned her back on him and stomped out with her Pekinese dog under her arm. I was just embarrassed to tears. I didn't know what to say. Poor old Harry. She had a reputation for doing this kind of thing, but that did- n't make any it easier when it hit."

Jack's next turn on his financial roller-coaster was once again cut short by powers beyond his control. He wanted to build a full bar and found a wealthy partner to finance it. He and a helper then built the big log building that now houses Dornan's grocery store. "I'll never for- get it!" Bob exclaims. "On December 6, 1941, they put the top log on that building. On December 7, the Japanese bombed Pearl Harbor. All assets in the Philippines were frozen. Dad's partner's money was in the Philippines. He was a millionaire one day and broke the next. The building was left unfinished. Dad could see that there wouldn't be much tourism during the war, and he was very upset by the attack on Pearl Harbor. So he locked up everything and went to work as a pur- chasing agent for Morrison-Knudsen, a naval gun plant in Pocatello, Idaho, and he worked for them all during the war."

As he had in his job in California, Jack did very well at Morrison- Knudsen. By the end of the war, the company offered him a vice pres- idency in San Francisco, heading up their foreign operations. "Dad was really torn between taking this big job and going back to Jackson Hole. Finally, he said, 'We'll take the summer off and go up and see if we can sell the place.' He was actually going to sell his property up here. And he got an offer on it, too. This guy came up and was interested in buying it. Dad told him he wanted $33,500 for it. The guy said, 'All right. I'll be back tomorrow to sign the papers.' And he never showed up. Mother said, 'Well, I really didn't want to leave here.' Dad said, 'Ah, to hell with it. I'm going to keep it.' So he finished that big log building that got stopped by World War II and went on with the business."

The postwar years were good for Jack. He was finally on firm ground and moving steadily ahead with his business. In 1948, he added the landmark Original Chuckwagon restaurant, complete with tipis, which still serves its Dutch oven outdoor cooking and sourdough pancake breakfasts. By the 1950s he also had a thriving grocery store and a bar with a liquor license. The bar was squeezed into the present grocery store building, where the deli counter now is, and it had the usual small bar window despite the fabulous view outside. But wine was going to change all that.

"This was when all the eastern dudes came to the ranches here," Bob explains. "They said, 'Jack, why don't you get some wine in? We like wine, and it's a hassle to bring it out west.' A big lightbulb went on in Dad's head, and he went right to work." Twenty years later, the wine business was so extensive that the family borrowed a large sum of money to build The Wine Shoppe plus the current bar and restaurant with its big windows for the Teton view. "And we basically did all this," laughs Bob, "because we needed more space for the wine."

Jack was winning the battle with turbulent finances, but now another battle was intensifying. On September 14, 1950, Grand Teton National Park as we now know it was officially created. Dornan's in Moose was situated inside the Park, and some officials wanted the land sold to the park and the buildings removed or demolished. Jack staunchly refused to sell, and park officials equally staunchly refused to take his "No!" for an answer.

"Dad never backed off from a fight," his son Bob points out. "And he was friends with some powerful politicians. I remember one instance. The park superintendent was sort of a hard-core guy. He and his chief ranger came in one night and said they wanted to talk to Dad. I happened to be there with him. This superintendent says, 'Mr. Dornan, you'd better sell us this property because if you don't, we're going to condemn it and take it away from you.' Boy, I thought Dad would pull out his six-shooter and shoot the guy. But he really amazed me. He was very calm. He just said, 'Fine, I wish you a lot of luck.' Then, when the guy had walked out the door, Dad said, 'I'm going to show that S.O.B.' And he got on the phone and called his political friends."

Jack won that round. And he won other rounds after that. As Ellen Dornan quietly explained to the Jackson Hole Historical Society and Museum, "It has been observed that the Park didn't know Jack had as much power as he did with the politicians to fight them." In fervent opposition to Ellen's father, J. R. Jones, Jack was fiercely opposed to Grand Teton National Park and especially when it threatened his hard-

Evelyn Dornan at about age seventy, c. 1950. Courtesy of the Dornan family.

won business and property. "I think, mainly, it was a personal thing," Ellen said. "He had gone through a lot with his parents pulling different ways when he was a child in the East. There was no feeling of close family life. Jack had a feeling of freedom out here and didn't want it encroached upon in any way. He felt he had established this freedom. He became a very strong individual and, as a whole, a very fair person. However, if someone tried to push him, he was a fighter."

It was while Jack was fighting to keep his property from being taken by the park that his mother struck a stunning blow. She sold her half of the property to the park in 1952. She sold to her son's major enemy, as he saw it, and to the one owner from whom he could never buy back the property. "I'm still upset about it," says Bob. "Because I remember, Dad went down and talked to her one day. She was getting on in years. She must have been seventy-one by then. Dad said, 'I'd like to buy your half of the place,' and out of the blue she said, 'I've already sold it to the park.' "

"It always struck me as ironic," Evelyn's grandson Dave muses, "that she spent her life ranting against the government and being critical of government growth and power, yet she cooperated with them when it came to selling her land to the National Park Service. This was done secretly, and in large part I think it was done to spite my Dad. At the time she sold her property, my Dad needed more land and could have bought it from her. The underlying animosity toward her own son and her betrayal of the family on the land sale issue was the final straw for all of us; I don't think we could ever forgive her after that."

Jack persevered in building his business on his remaining property, and he succeeded despite his battle with the park. After more than twelve years, he was still winning, but it was still a battle. By the mid-1960s, Jack had built a bar addition and enlarged his grocery store and deli. One day a man he did not know walked into his place. The man did not look like a tourist.

"He was nosing around," says Bob, "and Dad didn't know who he was or anything else. He spent a day or two coming in and checking things out. Dad didn't run him off the property. He must have been in a good mood. Finally, the man came up and introduced himself to Dad. 'Mr. Dornan,' he says, 'I want to compliment you. I'm George Hartzog, Director of the National Park Service.' Dad did a sort of double-take and said, 'All right, what can I do for you?' "

"He said, 'Mr. Dornan, I congratulate you. I've been checking your prices, and you're selling your wares a lot cheaper than our Park concessionaires do. You're giving the tourists a good deal. We appreciate that.' That was a complete change of attitude of the Park from all the previous years. He and Dad actually became good friends after that. He would stop by every year and come visit with Dad. And Dad would go to Washington about every other year, and he'd stop in and visit with him there. And on the whole, after

Group photo from the movie Spencer's Mountain, 1963. Bit player Virginia Dornan stands behind movie stars Maureen O'Hara and Henry Fonda.

that, we got along very well with the park."

In the 1950s, the Dornan children were growing up and Ellen was learning to drive. With more free time, she became active in the community and worked with St. John's Hospital. She was an original founder of the Fine Arts Guild, which supported the Jackson Hole Symphony at Teton Village. She was invited to President Eisenhower's inauguration in recognition of her work as Vice President of Republican Women in Wyoming. She loved her daily walks, her luncheons were famous, and she was known as a formidable bridge player.

She and her daughter, Virginia, were bit players in the 1963 Hollywood movie, Spencer's Mountain, filmed in Jackson Hole, and photos in Dornan's bar show them with stars Henry Fonda and Maureen O'Hara.

In the spring of 1965, Evelyn Dornan died. She was eighty-three

Bit player Ellen Dornan is third from the right. Courtesy of the Dornan family.

years old and had been ill for some time in a Colorado nursing home. Jack and Ellen were with her at the end. Years after her death, pondering her influence on his life, her grandson Dave wrote of her,

> She was very self-centered and opinionated. She did nothing to celebrate us children. She fought continually with my father and treated my mother as though she were beneath her.
>
> Yet, despite these negative memories, I have to admit that I benefited in knowing Gran from those summers she spent in the Tetons. Visiting her house was always a treat, because it was filled with things that I never saw anyplace else. She had a large Chinese screen in her living room; she had sea shells, vases, and art pieces, all of which spoke of faraway places or the ocean (which I had never seen). From Gran I learned that there was a different way to live; the world didn't have to be all hard work and struggle. I saw that there was a more gracious life style and that education made a difference. She showed me that it is important to appreciate nature and to honor those people who work as naturalists. She made me aware that we have a Quaker family history.

In 1972, Jack and Ellen retired, and their sons took over the Dornan business. Jack could now indulge in one of his lifelong loves, playing golf. He joined a number of country clubs and played both in the U.S. and abroad. He and Ellen spent their winters primarily in Arizona, returning to their house in Moose for the summers. "He had a great deal of warmth which became apparent in his later years when he had time to sort things out and wasn't so pressured in making a living," Ellen said of those years together.

He was playing in the Pro Am Invitational Golf Tournament in Mexico when he was stricken with heart failure and died peacefully on

November 30, 1978. Even though Ellen lived on for another twenty-two years, he did indeed occupy most of her life, as she had said he would. Of their life together she said, "Jack was a character, an individual, and people admired what he stood for and what he accomplished. He had a wonderful proportion of things to do with construction and, more importantly, with everyday living. His never-ceasing love and understanding of me was always a strong support. We had our 51st wedding anniversary before he passed away." For most of the rest of her life, she continued to spend winters in Arizona and summers with her family in Jackson Hole.

And Dornan's in Moose continued to prosper. The distinctive new Spur Ranch Cabins, created and managed by his son Rod, replaced Jack's old log cabins. When Bob Dornan retired, Dick and Tricia, his brother and sister-in-law, took over the running of the business. Fourth generation Dornans grew up and took part in the business.

Ellen Dornan died in Moose in the spring of 2001, lovingly cared

for by her son Rod and his wife, Carol. She was ninety-seven years old. Her life was rich and often hard, and it was deeply rooted in Jackson Hole, where she lived for

Ellen Dornan at about age ninety-three, four years before her death, c. 1997. Courtesy of the Dornan family.

ninety-three years. Her family wrote of her, "Her spirit was indomitable. She was strong and remarkably gentle considering the hardship. Her children recall her strength and unconditional devotion to their lives. Her nephew remembers that 'Aunt Ellen's dignity and elegance in the face of a variety of hardships and trials were always an inspiration.' " She is buried beside Jack in the Aspen Hill Cemetery in Jackson.

Today, Dornan's in Moose has been in business for fifty-six years and serves about three million Grand Teton National Park visitors every year. Most of its facilities are open year-round and offer winter as well as summer visitors some unique experiences in the park. Despite its more modern conveniences, Dornan's in Moose still retains the old Western atmosphere that Jack Dornan first created.

In a sense, Jack Dornan made an honest woman of his mother. She homesteaded in Jackson Hole under false pretenses. But on this small acreage where real homesteading was impossible, Jack created a genuine Western establishment that serves the public well and has its roots in Jackson Hole history. "We deliver a good job to the tourists," says Bob Dornan. "I think that is what I really call my grandmother and my Dad's legacy, what they started and we still carry on. I'm very proud of that, and I think it's a good legacy to hold on to. Hopefully, some of our kids will carry it on in the future."

CHAPTER NINE

ALBERT AND LIDA GABBEY

ARRIVED IN JACKSON HOLE IN 1924

⊱⊹⊙⊹⊰

THE Cathedral Group Scenic Turnout in Grand Teton National Park is one of the most beautiful locations in Jackson Hole. From there, Teewinot Mountain, the Grand Teton, and Mount Owen appear as cathedral-like spires. Thus the name of the turnout. About 500 yards east and a little north of the turnout was the boundary of the Square G Ranch, famous in its day for its matchless views and warm, easygoing hospitality.

Many of the original Square G cabins are now part of Colter Bay Village. All that remains of the ranch in its original location are some hints of a road, a fire circle, the old dump, and occasional pieces of concrete, metal, and glass. After fifty years, these signs of the once thriving guest ranch are obscure, but you can find them if you look.

Albert and Lida Gabbey homesteaded the Square G Ranch in 1927. At that time, homesteading was coming to an end in Jackson Hole, but meanwhile Henry Ford's mass production of cars had launched a new travel and vacation era, and the Square G Ranch would become a symbol of one of the best destinations of its time.

When the Gabbeys started building their guest cabins, the revolution spawned in 1909 by the Model T Ford was well underway. In

1916, Congress passed the Federal Aid Road Act, which provided $75,000,000 for highway construction, and by 1921 the interstate system of highways was well underway. By 1930, there were 23 million cars in the U.S., and America's love affair with the automobile was in full swing. Middle class Americans roamed their country by car, setting the patterns of modern tourism. Dude ranchers in Jackson Hole called them tin-can tourists. They were central characters in the era that changed the valley from a community dependent on cattle ranching to one based on tourism.

The beginning of Jackson Hole tourism was mixed and busy. According to Jackson Hole historian John Daugherty, "Along the road to Jenny Lake businesses blossomed to cater to the automobile traffic." Some, like the Elbo Ranch, were gaudy. It had "tourist cabins, a store, a baseball diamond, and a large rodeo ground complete with race track, grandstands, and refreshment kiosks." A huge sign announced it as "the home of the Hollywood Cowboy." Others, like the Square G Ranch, honored their beautiful environment and built facilities where visitors could enjoy it without spoiling it.

Albert Gabbey called the Square G a guest ranch to distinguish it from a dude ranch. The two were different in both history and practice. Traditional dude ranches usually evolved from old cattle ranches, and many operated as both. They accepted guests by reservation only and some even required references before they would accept a guest. They refused walk-in traffic such as tin-can tourists who might want to stop for a night or two before they drove on. They offered the American Plan only, a package price for lodging, food, and horseback riding.

The Square G Ranch had no previous connection to cattle ranching and no cattle. It offered cabins with maid service and á la carte meals in the dining room. It also offered housekeeping cabins where guests could cook their own food. Walk-in guests were welcome. Local people were welcome to come to the dining room for a meal, and many did so. The Square G Ranch offered horseback riding, and as close as it was to the Tetons and Jenny, String, and Leigh Lakes, it also offered mountain guides and boats.

Successful Jackson Hole dude ranches had a unique personality, recognized and appreciated by their clientele. The Square G Ranch had its own character, as unique as that of the classic dude ranch, the Bar BC. Like the Bar BC, the Square G drew its personality from its creators and owners, Albert and Lida Gabbey. Or, as they were affectionately called by guests and staff, "Mr. and Mrs. Square G."

Compared with other Jackson Hole homesteaders, the Gabbeys were relatively old when they homesteaded and built the Square G Ranch. Of middle age, they both had careers behind them when they began their new profession as guest ranch owners. Lida was a schoolteacher from Missouri who had gone on to teach in Rigby, Idaho. Albert grew up in Kansas and came to Rigby in 1919, where he became a successful businessman. He actively promoted the Beet Growers Sugar Company, which built a major sugar mill in the area.

Albert and Lida were married in Rigby in 1922. After several years of going camping in Jackson Hole, they decided to move there. By the

The Square G Guest Ranch, pictured here in the 1930s, differed in many ways from the traditional dude ranch. For one thing, it welcomed "tin-can" tourists, who arrived by car in increasing numbers. Jackson Hole Historical Society and Museum, 2005.0045.037.

winter of 1925, they had wound up their business connections in Rigby and were living in Kelly before moving on to the Jenny Lake area, where they had filed for a homestead near String Lake. Lida taught school at Jenny Lake, and she was also appointed its first postmaster. Albert leased a site by the dirt and gravel highway and built the first store at Jenny Lake. This was their financial base while they proved up on their homestead. Albert's store was eventually rolled on logs through the snow to its new home on the Square G Ranch.

The Gabbeys received their homestead patent for the Square G in 1932 and went to work full scale to complete the ranch. Bob Kranenberg, who helped build the ranch and became its foreman, remembers that time. "We laid up the logs for the guest cabins, and we peeled only the part of the log that would go on the inside and left the bark on the outside, which made our cabins kind of unique. We had lots of trees, but we didn't cut any down. Most people go in and just

"Mr. and Mrs. Square G" in front of Albert Gabbey's ranch office, c. 1940. Jackson Hole Historical Society and Museum, 2003.0117.419.

clear everything. We didn't; we just trimmed the trees. Mr. Gabbey and I placed the cabins so they weren't in front of each other. Each cabin had its own view of the mountains. We also built everything inside each cabin except the bed springs and mattress and stove. Eventually, there were 31 cabins and a large main lodge."

The ranch buildings were about a mile and a half from String Lake, and for the first three years the ranch did not have a well. "I hauled all the water to the Square G in eight gallon milk cans and put one at each cabin," says Bob. Guests bathed in tin tubs in their cabins for four years until the ranch had a bathhouse with a shower.

The Square G brochure for 1934 features fully furnished log cabins with handmade lodgepole pine furniture. A one-room cabin was $2 to $2.50 per day and $12.50 to $16.50 per week. A three-room cabin was $4 per day and $25 per week. Breakfast in the dining room was á la carte; lunch was 50¢, and dinner was 75¢.

Lida Gabbey's nephew, Tom Lindley, worked at the Square G as a young man and met this wife, Ruth, there. "I came to Jackson to visit the Mercill family in the summer of 1936," Ruth recalls. "I was a young college student from the University of Minnesota. Edith Mercill invited me to the Square G Ranch for 4th of July dinner, and that was a delightful experience. I asked Mrs. Gabbey if she had any positions open. She did not. But early the next morning she phoned me. Someone had become ill in the middle of the night, and if I was still interested, please come out to the ranch. So I went bag and baggage, and that started five wonderful years on the Square G. The first summer I worked in the kitchen; I think I was replacing the dishwasher. But I didn't mind. I was delighted to be there. It was a great place, a very lovely place."

The next summer, Ruth was made second cook. "I was only 18 years old, but I jumped at the chance. Mrs. Gabby gave me some fundamental instructions so I could adapt quickly, because we were serving a dining room with large numbers of people."

Tom Lindley had a job at the ranch gas station. "My job started at 6 AM every morning, because people wanted an early start when they were leaving the ranch. And we kept open until 10 PM for the people who were coming in. That was a long day, and it was seven days a week. But I enjoyed every minute of it. I enjoyed every minute on the Square G."

That summer was the beginning of Tom and Ruth's romance. They were married at the Chapel of the Transfiguration in Moose at the end of their fifth summer at the Square G, and the Gabbeys hosted their wedding reception at the ranch.

"We saw the Square G grow," Ruth explains.

Originally, they took guests off the highway, and they always accommodated them if they could. But people began coming there from everywhere, and the business grew so rapidly that reservations eventually were booked years in advance by a lot of guests who came regularly. Most guests came by their own automobiles, interesting people from many colleges and universities. Some guests came from as far away as England.

The Gabbeys were quite exceptional people. They were recognized for being very hospitable, kind people, talented people, and wonderful to work for. Mr. Gabbey was very definitely a business man, and Mrs. Gabbey was equal to him in her capacity. Mr. Gabbey handled the financial end and all the reservations for the ranch. Mrs. Gabbey was totally in charge of hiring the staff. There were quite a few. She also had full charge of the dining room and responsibility for ordering all of the food, a lot of which came from Salt Lake City. They divided their responsibilities. They shared their philosophy. It was their philosophy that built the ranch.

Bob Kranenberg remembers Mr. Gabbey getting up at 5:30 every morning. "He had a little old office not much bigger than my kitchen table, and he had all the paper work. Believe me, it was a lot of paper work. He typed very efficiently with one finger on each hand, and he'd have it all done by 7:30 and have breakfast with us."

Top: Lida and Albert Gabbey on the Square G in the 1930s. Jackson Hole Historical Society and Museum, 1993.4892.011.

Left: As owner of the Square G, Albert Gabbey was a warm and humorous "guest wrangler," c. 1940. He could also be tough when he needed to defend the ranch. Jackson Hole Historical Society and Museum, 1958.1997.001.

Everything was going well for the Square G Ranch until the General Land Office denied Albert Gabbey's second stock-raising homestead entry, a common way for homesteaders to expand their land holdings. Similar Jackson Hole stock-raising entries had been

Dudes riding on the Square G Ranch in front of the Cathedral Group of the Tetons, c. 1940. Jackson Hole Historical Society and Museum, 2005.0128.001.

approved, so why was Albert Gabbey turned down? Because of behind-the-scenes maneuvering by the National Park Service, whose agents regularly challenged the validity of pending Jackson Hole homestead entries and believed that many were "fraudulent and not in good faith."

This was possibly true in some cases, but not in the case of Albert Gabbey, who was in compliance with the law. Nevertheless, in response to pressure from park service officials, the General Land Office rejected Albert Gabbey's stock-raising entry on the grounds that the land was not classifiable as stock-raising. This was questionable, since Gabbey's immediate neighbor, the painter and photographer Harrison Crandall, had no trouble getting his stock-raising entry approved. Albert Gabbey had to fight for thirteen years to secure his rights. He finally won, on the indisputable grounds that the law had been applied inconsistently. His case became part of the valley's arguments for and against the establishment of Grand Teton National Park.

"Mr. Gabbey was a very strong, very fascinating, intelligent man. And he had a great sense of humor," says Ruth Lindley. He inspired a number of stories.

One of the famous Square G stories was about him. We had a big bear population on the ranch. Almost every evening they would come down to the back porch, where there were some metal garbage cans. In those days, Mr. Gabbey always wore a night shirt. This was his night attire. Also, he never went anywhere without his ten-gallon hat. It was so much fun, because the bears would come to maraud the garbage cans, and he would get up out of his bed, put on his night shirt and his hat and come out with his gun to shoot at those bears. He didn't kill them. He only scared them away, because the Gabbeys were very humane people. It was always a funny story, and it was drawn up in cartoons by guests at the ranch.

The atmosphere at the Square G was very relaxed. This is where the Square G was preferable to a dude ranch, in Bob Kranenberg's opinion. "The Gabbeys let guests do what they wanted and didn't try to herd them around." Guests were free to go horseback riding when they chose, with or without a guide and often all the way up Cascade Canyon to Lake Solitude. The ranch had a corral where the horses gathered in the morning. "Curly was in charge of the horses," Ruth recalls, "and he was the most colorful of cowboys." "Curly was also a singer," Tom adds. "Every chance he got, he would serenade the ranch. He could have been a professional singer. But he would rather be a cowboy."

"Did I tell you about the little four-year-old girl at the corral?" asks Bob. "She was the daughter of the couple who ran the horse concession on the ranch, and could she ride those horses! If guests couldn't handle a horse, she would get right up on it and show them how to ride. Four years old. They had to lift her onto the horse. She was the cutest thing, and she wasn't afraid of anything."

Many guests liked to go fishing in the nearby lakes. They could order box lunches to take with them. The guests often became interested in the operation of the ranch. "They were known to get right out and help with building or help logging or chopping wood. It was simply a matter of interest on their part," says Ruth. "The guests were also friendly to the staff. They would go with us to town for rodeos, and always on Saturday nights."

The relaxed atmosphere of the Square G drew local people to it. Some would stay for awhile; others would frequent the dining room. The painter Archie Teater camped at the ranch in his Jeep while painting the Tetons. He painted them so often and so successfully that he acquired the nickname "Teton Teater." The celebrated climber Glenn Exum, for whom a main route up the Grand Teton is named, would come with other climbers for meals. Perhaps the most exotic guests were Reginald and Gladys Laubin, international performers of Native

American dances who also wrote and illustrated books on Native American tipis, dances, and archery. Before the Laubins built their home in Moose, they would stay at the Square G, raise their tipi outside their cabin, and dance for guests and staff.

The Square G had a handsome main lodge with a dining room extending out from the lodge. Both were entirely furnished with furniture that was handmade on the ranch. "The end of the dining room

The multitalented Gladys and Reginald Laubin perform at the Square G, c. 1940. Photo courtesy of Bob Kranenberg.

framed the Cathedral Group of mountains. And many artists hung their paintings there," Ruth recalls.

It was a lovely room. Mrs. Gabbey had a very pleasing eye for the finishing touches. There were wild flowers on every table, every day. And the china and glassware were colorful.

They took great pride in the food they served. And, amazingly, they did all their cooking and baking for their guests and for the staff on a wood range. A big, hotel-size wood range. One of Mrs. Gabbey's requirements was that there were homemade hot rolls every day for lunch, and all the desserts were homemade, too. She would go into town every day for the rest of the bread, which she bought in a bakery that was where the Buffalo Trail Gallery is now. One of the interesting things I remember is that all of the milk, cream, and butter came from Bartha Moulton on Mormon Row. She would come every day, bringing those supplies. We got to know her pretty well. And when it was huckleberry season, she would come with huckleberries. Mrs. Gabbey was warm and sweet. I found her extremely understanding and unusually joyful for the amount of cares and responsibilities she had. A very intelligent woman.

During the winter, the Square G would be closed, but for some years the Gabbeys stayed through the cold and the snow. Bob Kranenberg would snowshoe down to Moose for the mail, and he would shovel a lot of snow. An avid photographer, he took many photographs of the Square G. "This is one of the cabins I was shoveling off. The stove pipe is over five feet, and the snow is right up there. And that snow was really icy with lots of weight. Sometimes I'd have to shovel all the cabins off two or three times a winter."

Winter did bring peace and quiet after the busy summers, and

Top: Deep winter with snowshoe tracks on the Square G Ranch, c. 1950. Photo courtesy of Bob Kranenberg.

Left: Bob Kranenberg saws and shovels ice and snow off of a Square G cabin in 1952. There were thirty-one cabins and the main lodge to shovel on the ranch. Jackson Hole Historical Society and Museum, 1993.4773. 011.

Top: Lida Gabbey in the doorway of a typical Square G cabin in winter, c. 1930s. Jackson Hole Historical Society and Museum, 1993.4779.011. Bottom: Even when he went ice fishing, Albert Gabbey wore his ten-gallon hat, 1931. Jackson Hole Historical Society and Museum, 2003.0117.174.

there was time for getting together with friends. The Gabbeys and their neighbors, the Crandalls, got together for holidays like Thanksgiving and Christmas, and there were parties where they played poker all night. Lida Gabbey was close friends with Geraldine Lucas, who frequently came up to the ranch with her dogsled team. "Lida and Geraldine were similar in their intellect. They enjoyed literature of all kinds. They shared many a winter day, I think," says Ruth. "Lida also did extensive needlework in the winter. There are many examples of her work. One of them I've seen in the history museum in Jackson. It's a quilt made by a group of local women. They each did a block on the quilt and signed it. Lida was social; she loved companionship, and she had many friends in the valley."

Albert Gabbey led an active life with the Democratic Party. For several years, he was chairman of the Teton County committee, and he was a delegate to the Democratic national convention.

With advancing age, the Gabbeys wintered in Twenty-Nine Palms, California, while Bob Kranenberg was caretaker of the ranch. But every spring, they returned to the Square G, which was always booked solid for the summer.

Suddenly, in the fall of 1947, Albert Gabbey died of a heart attack. His death shocked his family and the Jackson Hole community. "He had not been ill. He was a very active man," said Ruth. The Jackson Hole newspaper wrote, "He had spent part of the previous day visiting and on business, apparently in his usual health." The family held funeral services at the Chapel of the Transfiguration in Moose. A large number of Wyoming friends followed his body to Rigby, where he was buried in the Pioneer Cemetery.

For three years after Albert's death, Lida continued to run the Square G. "It was a big load for her," says Ruth, "but she did ably. However, her health was failing, and she felt the time had come to sell." In the fall of 1951, Lida sold the Square G Ranch to the Jackson Hole Preserve, John D. Rockefeller, Jr.'s company, which then gave it to the

National Park Service. "It was very sad and a big loss," Ruth continues, "but that's exactly what happened."

Right to the end, the ranch kept its unique personality. Most tourist facilities were being modernized as fast as possible. Not the Square G. Rod Newcomb, who was a dishwasher there in the summer of 1953, reminisces, "Log cabins, home-made lodgepole pine furniture, wood stoves, real ice boxes with ice from the icehouse, milk cans filled with water from the Fairbanks-Morse single-piston pump, kerosene lamps, and outhouses . . ."—this was the Square G.

"Our power at the ranch was from a 6 kilowatt Kohler power plant," he continues.

Lida Gabbey, c. 1940. Jackson Hole Historical Society and Museum, 1958.1998.001.

There was just enough power to run the walk-in refrigerator, a small freezer, and lights in the bath house, kitchen, dining room, and lights in the manager's wing of the lodge. When [the manager] turned on her iron, the lights dimmed and the power plant slowed down. The power plant was cranked on at 6:00 a.m. and usually turned off at 10:00 p.m. I became painfully aware of this on my first night of work. I had washed every dish and pan from the dining room and kitchen, and scrubbed the kitchen floor. I needed a shower. Halfway through the shower, on a moonless night, the power plant turned off. It took some doing to gather up and feel my way back to the boys' cabin.

Lida Gabbey died in 1961 and was buried beside her husband in Rigby. The house she built on the Square G after Albert died, and filled with the furniture and memorabilia he made, is now Tom and Ruth Lindley's summer home north of Wilson.

Although the times and the setting are different, many Square G buildings live on in Colter Bay Village. The old Square G store became the Colter Bay cabin office. The main lodge with Lida's dining room and Albert Gabbey's office became the Colter Bay guest lounge, and the icehouse became the Colter Bay housekeeping office. Today many Colter Bay guests stay in original Square G guest cabins that were renovated in 1959.

And, still, the memories linger. "We are very fortunate to have known and been part of the Square G Ranch," Ruth and Tom agree. "We learned a lot. We learned from the guests, fascinating people from all walks of life. We learned about business management and human relations and great respect for the land. It was wonderful to have known Mr. and Mrs. Square G. Sometimes we go up to Colter Bay Village, where most of the Square G cabins were moved in 1956. We know where they are, and we can identify a lot of them."

"I have very warm memories of my time at the Square G," says Rod Newcomb. "And it was there I first came to appreciate the Tetons. I wondered if I could climb them." Now seventy, this longtime mountaineer is co-owner of the Exum Mountain Guides in Jackson Hole and Director of the American Avalanche Institute. Fifty-one years after his summer at the Square G, Rod went back and found the old site. "My trip to the Square G site brought back memories of a small part of the world and a slower, less complicated way of life. Being at the Square G was a touch of living in the 'Old West.' "

CHAPTER TEN

EVA AND FRED TOPPING

ARRIVED IN JACKSON HOLE IN 1927

O F all Jackson Hole's historic dude ranches, only a few are still operating. One of them is the beautiful Moose Head Ranch in Grand Teton National Park. It was homesteaded by a woman, and she made it hers just in the nick of time.

Eva Grace Sanford came from two generations of Wyoming homesteaders. Her grandparents left Iowa in 1882, when the Army employed her grandfather as a blacksmith and carpenter at Fort Fetterman near Douglas. They had just married, and their trip west in a covered wagon was their honeymoon. They lived on their homestead into old age, and their three daughters were born and grew up there.

As Eva did, her mother had homesteaded her own place. "Women could homestead when they were 21 if they were not married," Eva explained to the Jackson Hole Historical Society and Museum in an interview about her life. "Mother didn't have any intentions of getting married at the time she was 21, so she claimed 160 acres near my grandparents' ranch. When she and my father were married, she already had the homestead."

Eva was born on her mother's homestead in 1903. She and her sister and two brothers grew up like most children on western home-steads, as working partners with their parents. "We children worked to put food on the table. We would all help milk the cows, and we had the pigs to feed and the chickens to feed. The buildings had to be cleaned. In the summer time, we were all farming." Farming near Douglas was even more difficult than in Jackson Hole. "We didn't have many cattle. That land over by Douglas is all barren land like Rock Springs. It takes 40 acres for one cow. It's good feed, but they just have to roam and roam for what they get—a bit here and a bit there out in the sagebrush."

At that time, if you were cash poor and lived twenty to thirty miles from the nearest small town, there was only one way of getting an education: you left home and worked your way through school. Eva did this. It taught her self-reliance, hard work, and making use of whatever became available. These traits served her well and would help her build the Moose Head Ranch.

"When I was 13 years old, I went on my own as far as cash was concerned. I started working out. I worked for my grandmother in the summertime. Then I graduated from that and went to work for other people in the summertime to earn money to go to school with. When I got ready for high school, I just made my own way."

She left home and went to high school in Glenrock, where her wid-owed aunt had a hotel. For two years, she worked for her for room and board while going to school. "I worked morning and night. I'd get to bed about midnight and have to get up about 5:00 to help get breakfast. Saturday and Sunday we did the laundry, cleaning, and ironing with hand irons heated on the stove. Then one of the teachers and his moth-er, who had a big nice house there in town, wanted me to go to work for them. They paid me $20 a month, so I took that and got away from my aunt, because I was getting up in high school where I needed a little per-sonal money for myself." Eva never felt sorry for herself. Of her child-hood and its hardships, she said, "I think it was a good, clean life."

At that time, the only place in Wyoming to get a full teacher's certificate was at the University of Wyoming in Laramie. But the state of Wyoming permitted high schools to give one year of teacher's training, which was equal to the first year at the university. So Eva continued at Glen Rock high school and graduated with a certificate to teach in rural schools.

"I applied to teach at Moorcroft, near Newcastle, and one north of Douglas, out in that God-forsaken country where there wasn't even a jack rabbit. The other one I applied to was up here in Teton County. I investigated on the map, and I knew it was real beautiful. I was real tired of where I grew up, and I didn't want to get stuck there for the rest of my life and maybe marry somebody and do dry farming. I felt there was something more beautiful, at least." Teton County offered her not only beauty but also more money than the two other counties, $90 a month plus $5 janitor fees. This was her chance for something better, and she grabbed it.

Eva Sanford, the young Spread Creek teacher, with Margaret Cunningham, c. 1924. Jackson Hole Historical Society and Museum, 1958.1775.001.

In September of 1924, Eva's parents drove her to Jackson Hole in their old Model T Ford. Eva was fond of telling the story of coming over Togwotee Pass and getting her first view of the Tetons and Jackson Hole. She told her parents that she was sure she would spend the rest of her life there, because it was so beautiful. She was twenty-one years old, and she did indeed spend the rest of her life in Jackson Hole.

Her school was in the neighborhood of what is now the Cunningham Cabin Historic Site in Grand Teton National Park, and she boarded with the Cunninghams. She started with twelve children, then sixteen, and for three years she taught eight grades. One year, she also taught ninth grade on her own time, without extra pay. "There were four eighth grade girls that couldn't go on to the ninth grade because there was no school. I taught them the ninth grade free, just so they could go to school."

And then in 1927 she became a homesteader. This step was not part of her plan, but it became possible and so she adopted it. "The neighbors around there found out that there were 120 acres that were never homesteaded. The land was pocketed—other ranches were fenced in around it—and nobody owned it. At the time, I didn't know what it would be good for, but they suggested that I homestead. So I did, in May. It was already fenced, so I didn't have to do that, and I had five years to build a cabin and plow up 20 acres and look like I was going to make a home there. It was all swamps and cobble rocks and willows, but it had a beautiful view!"

Shortly after acquiring her land, Eva married Fred Topping, a neighbor in the area whose wife had died in a flu epidemic during World War I. Complementing Eva in both personality and skills, Fred became her invaluable partner in creating one of Jackson Hole's longest running dude ranches.

Fred Topping was born in 1883 in a little village in Quebec, Canada. When he was two years old, his father, mother, and eight siblings moved to New Hampshire, where his mother died. His father-married another French Canadian woman, and they settled in Lawrence, Massachusetts. Here, Fred had to learn English and go to school. At age sixteen, like most of the children of poor families in Lawrence, he went to work in a woolen mill. He also worked for the Lawrence Ice Company, cutting blocks of ice from the lakes. And in Lawrence he got his first taste of working with horses, something he would cherish and that would become an important part of his life. The ice delivery wagons were pulled by Percheron horses. Later, at the Lawrence Fire Department, he also worked with Percheron teams. When he went west at the age of twenty-four, he carried photos of those fine horses with him.

Fred and his friend George Greenwood had been reading about the West, and they decided that this was the place for them. Eva described their adventure. "They wanted the West real tough and wild

Fred Topping on horseback, n.d. Jackson Hole Historical Society and Museum, 1958.3122.001.

and woolly, so they went to the end of the railroad in Wyoming. That was Lander. Work there was scarce, so George got on the stage and went on to Pinedale. Fred stayed around Lander and worked on ranches with teams and breaking horses. The wilder the better. Lander was only a wide place in the street then, rough and tough. Times were hard and life wasn't easy. So the West lived up to his expectations and dreams."

In 1912, Fred decided to come to Jackson Hole. He had heard that Jackson Hole's first rodeo was being organized and brought rodeo stock over Union Pass. He liked the valley so much that he homesteaded near Elk, Wyoming, where Eva would later have her homestead. He developed a hunting guide business, working with the White Grass Ranch and Ben Sheffield's lodge and outfitting business in Moran. In 1916, he married. In 1918, he was a widower. He also sold his homestead that year, but he still considered the Spread Creek area his home.

He became an independent outfitter, guiding hunting pack-trips of three to six weeks in areas from the Gros Ventre mountains up into most of Yellowstone National Park. He was guide, cook, and horse wrangler, and he worked day and night on the long trips. When he retired in 1967 at age eighty-four, he was the oldest guide in Wyoming and had been guiding for the most years.

During his early times as an outfitter, Fred also had other kinds of work—like acting in the first movie filmed in Jackson Hole. This was in 1922, when *The Cowboy and the Lady*, starring the famous Hollywood ingenue Mary Miles Minter, was being filmed on the Gros Ventre River north of Jackson. Fred had a bit part playing an eastern dude. Acting was not new for Fred, who had spent a good deal of time on the stage, singing and dancing in vaudeville acts in Boston. As a dude rancher later in his life, he joked about his movie part, saying that for three days in his life *he* was the dude.

In 1927, newlyweds Fred and Eva Topping moved into an abandoned cabin on her 120 acres, and started clearing the land. "There was no machinery in those days such as tractors or pickup trucks or chain saws," Eva explained. "It was all done the hard, pioneer way. It was grazing land, a lot of swamp and willows, and with Spread Creek nearby, it was all cobble rock. If you plowed your top soil from two to five inches deep, when you turned it bottom side up, it was cobble rock so you couldn't even walk on it. So all this had to be worked by hand or with a team. Clearing it by hand, we made a ranch out of it." They worked on the homestead along with Fred's hunting business, which brought in enough cash to keep them going.

"When we started the Moose Head Ranch on my homestead, we named the place the Moose Head Ranch because it was the natural winter place for the moose. At the time I came here in 1924," Eva continued, "the moose were just starting to come to the area from Canada, across Montana, little by little. They drift, you know. When we'd feed

A Paramount Pictures publicity photo for its 1922 movie, The Cowboy and the Lady, in which Fred Topping got to play a dude. Jackson Hole Historical Society and Museum, 1958.3349.001.

the horses in the winter time, the moose would come into the feeding ground. One or two, then five or six, and they'd have their cows there and it was home to them. When we left the ranch in 1969, we fed 60 horses and just as many moose."

They cleared 30 acres for growing hay, and Fred had six horses for his guiding business. Then a neighbor gave them two heifer calves. "They just gave them away," Eva said, "because they were milking the cows and didn't want to feed the calves. Calves weren't worth anything in those

Feeding horses and moose in winter on the Moose Head Ranch, n.d. Photo by John Ryan. Courtesy of John and Marjorie Ryan.

days, you couldn't even get $5 apiece for them. Nobody wanted them."

These two calves turned out to be the start of Eva's dairy business. "They grew up with us. I fed them canned milk and they grew fat and sassy and spoiled. But they gave a lot of milk, so then I was in the butter business. I made butter and sold it to the neighbors and took it to town. Fred built a chicken coop and a barn the first thing. I had chickens and took the eggs and butter to the store. We hardly ever had to pay cash for groceries, just traded out. We didn't need much of anything that we couldn't produce ourselves, only flour, sugar, salt, and coffee. For those, we had to go into Jackson, maybe twice a year."

Their first home was a two-room cabin where they created a kitchen, bedroom, and parlor thanks to Fred's clever carpentry and Eva's curtains, sewed on her new Montgomery Ward sewing machine. For their food, they relied on Fred's hunting and on Eva's canning and gardening. "I canned everything at the ranch—elk meat, chickens, pork, and fish. I also canned all the wild greens I could find, and I had a big garden. You never saw a head of lettuce in a store. You grew your own."

Everything was going well for the Toppings until the homestead law stepped into their lives. The year 1927 was a troublesome one in which to homestead, as Eva had done. That year, President Calvin Coolidge issued a series of executive orders that withdrew thousands of acres from homesteading. Executive Order 4685 now threatened Eva's homestead. The Land Office protested her entry, and in August 1930 it sent an inspector out to investigate her claim. If it did not pass his examination, Eva might not get the patent to her land, and all their hard work would have been for nothing.

The inspector talked with people in the area to see if Eva had resided on her land for the required time and found that she had done so. He checked Fred and Eva's improvements on the land and found that they, too, met the requirements. His report stated that "From all evidence secured, I am of the opinion that the entrywoman has complied with the law both as to residence and improvements, and I therefore recommend that this case be clearlisted and passed to patent if otherwise found regular."

Eva was home free—except for the fact that she had married in 1927, and that her husband was a man who was born in Canada. That little phrase, "if otherwise found regular," now stood in the way of her patent. With her customary thoroughness, Eva set to work to meet the new legal requirements, and she was practical enough to get Wyoming's Senator Robert D. Carey to help her.

Legal forms and affidavits crossed the nation. The Commonwealth of Massachusetts supplied evidence that Fred Topping had been naturalized as a citizen of the United States on February 7, 1905. Eva went to the Teton County District Court, her marriage certificate in hand, to swear that she was the Eva Sanford who had filed her homestead claim in 1927, and that she was also the Eva Sanford who later had married Fred Topping. She had to sign her affidavit as both Eva G. Sanford and Eva G. Sanford Topping. That affidavit went off to the General Land Office. And Senator Carey wrote a letter to the General Land Office on Eva's behalf.

Finally, on December 22, 1931, the General Land Office officially declared that Eva's patent was on its way to her. The legal scramble had taken more than a year, and Christmas 1931 must have been extra merry for Eva and Fred. The land was now theirs, free and clear to do with as they pleased.

Their journey into successful dude ranching started with the arrival of what Eva called "the meat eaters," who evolved into their first paying customers. Moose Head Ranch was located on the elk migration trail, and hunters could hunt right from the ranch. One fall, the meat eaters started coming in from Rock Springs, Evanston, Rawlins, and Riverton to get their meat for the winter. Hunting was good, but there was no place for them to get even a cup of coffee. "The hunters would come up with a little old teepee and a lunch basket from home, figuring on making coffee out on the campfire, so we let them camp in our yard," Eva said.

I remember one time they came in November, and it was 20° below zero. Everything was covered with frost. Two groups of hunters came to my door and said, "Can we please come in? Would you fix us some breakfast? Everything we've got is frozen and we're so cold." I said, "Well, come on in. I haven't any facilities, but if you want to eat and can wait, I'll fix you breakfast." So I fixed them hotcakes and bacon and made them coffee.

Fred got the idea that if they wanted to come here, we'd better have a place for them. So he built a cabin or two and put an airtight heater in it, and beds, and then I started making quilts for the beds. We were absolutely self-reliant. We didn't buy anything. I made my own clothes and had some cuttings from sewing. So I'd spend the winters making quilts, and he'd build another cabin or two. He finally got a large cabin built, and we divided it into two rooms—a kitchen with the cookstove, and a dining room.

This went on for several years. The hunters came, twenty to thirty at a time, with their sleeping bags. They would be put up in the saddle house and cabin, and Eva would serve them breakfast and dinner. By midnight, she would usually finish washing the dishes and setting the table for next morning's breakfast.

Meanwhile, she was also a full-time postmaster. With the development of the Moose Head Ranch, the U.S. Postal Service added a post office at Elk and located it on the ranch. The job of postmaster in Jackson Hole was almost always held by women, and Elk was no exception. Of thirteen Elk postmasters between 1897 and 1968, ten were women. All were wives of local ranchers or, like Eva, were homesteaders themselves. Eva was appointed postmaster of Elk in 1933 and served for thirty-six years until they sold the ranch.

Then there was Eva and Fred and the Elk School. When the school was forced to move its building, Eva and Fred relocated it onto their property and leased it for free to the school district. One man who was a student there at the time recalled how Eva would invite all the students for Thanksgiving and Christmas dinner. "She had us up there at the old lodge. Dinner for the whole school. She was very nice to us kids who went to school there, and she was a great cook."

All this time, word of mouth was spreading the good news about the Moose Head Ranch. The resulting increase in visitors hit Eva unawares one freezing morning.

She recalls,

> I had the tables set up for our 20–25 guests. I had the coffee cups all set around and the whole bit ready. When I rang the bell for breakfast, it was 4:30 a.m. and pitch dark out there. A whole bunch of people I'd never seen before came into the house. And I said, "Where on earth did you people come from?" Half of them were already sitting at the tables. They said they'd been sitting in their trucks waiting for the breakfast bell and were half frozen. "Well," I said, "I don't mind you getting warm, but did it ever occur to you that this table is set for our guests? We have people in the cabins that want to eat. I didn't know you people were on earth, even." They said, well, they'd just leave, and I said, "You've messed the tables up, you might as well finish eating, then I'll get the others in."
>
> So I fed that gang of 12 or 15 people, then got the tables cleaned up, washed the dishes (I only had dishes enough for one setting), all by myself. But I had my hotcakes batter mixed up and my bacon cooked, and I managed to

serve our guests as they came in from the cabins. Somebody made hotcakes for me while I waited on the table, and I got that breakfast over with! Experiences like that with people were really something, and I loved every minute of it. I worked my head off, and I didn't have sense enough to go to bed at night, I had so much energy.

It was Fred's idea to start a dude ranch. He began to realize that there were people who wanted a place to stay in the summer. A nice,

Eva and Fred Topping out riding near their ranch, n.d. Jackson Hole Historical Society and Museum, 1958.0264.001.

simple place. A letter from a New York City sportswriter and his insurance broker friend set the tone: "We don't want anything fancy and if that is what you're offering, please tell us so and we'll drop the matter. We're young (24 and 26) but city-softened and in need of harding up. We want to ride and play rough; swim, but not in a pretty tile pool; eat, but not any French chef concoctions. We'll take steak, rare. We'd much prefer a pack trip, with a couple of nights in the open, to fishing."

The first dudes came in 1937, a man from Iowa City and a couple from Chicago. They kept coming back, others followed, and the dude ranch prospered.

Although Eva and Fred did not advertise, they did agree to have the Union Pacific describe the ranch in its brochure: "dining room and kitchen in one building; a ranch lobby; separate sleeping cabins of one and two rooms. Hot and cold tub and shower baths. Mrs. Topping is hostess and her garden and poultry department are show places. Ranch has its own dairy." Guests on the ranch could ride horses, fish, and hunt. Room, board and a saddle horse was $35 per week. "We built 40 log cabins up there," Eva recounted. "In later years we got help with them, because business kept coming in faster than Fred could build cabins by himself. We started taking families, and our business just came by word-of-mouth."

One family of guests was Mr. and Mrs. Maytag and their twin boys. One story told in the valley was about the time Fred was guiding the family way up Spread Creek, and Mrs. Maytag became quite ill. It looked like appendicitis. They tied her onto a saddle and brought her out of the hills on her horse, then sent word to Jackson to Dr. Huff, who came as far up the trail as he could drive in his pickup. After the operation was over, Mrs. Maytag told Fred that she had a lot better ride with him, tied on the saddle horse, than she did with Dr. Huff in that pickup.

Letters from returning families requesting reservations tended to be addressed "Dear Fred" and ran in the friendly way of the letter from

Top: Successful dude rancher Eva Topping stands by a Moose Head Ranch cabin, 1949. Jackson Hole Historical Society and Museum, 2005.0129.001. Bottom: Fred Topping and friend play guitar, n.d. Jackson Hole Historical Society and Museum, 1958.0256.001.

a lawyer in Illinois: "Some beautiful spring weather here the last few days has called my attention to the fact that summer probably is not far off, and the other members of the Taylor family are already shining up their boots and dusting off their hats for a trip to Wyoming. I imagine that quite a few other people around over the country are thinking about the same thing, so I thought I had better write you and see if I could make some reservations at the ranch for this summer."

Fred's lifelong friend George Greenwood had been working in Jackson Hole. "George was an excellent ax man," Eva related, "and whenever there was any timbering to be done, he was called upon to work the timber. There were no chain saws in those days, you had to work with an ax and hand saw. George cut many logs for many, many buildings. He had many friends. Many people respected him."

When Fred and Eva's ranch was beginning to prosper, George came and worked with them. His woodpile is still mentioned by old timers in Jackson Hole. Eva described it this way: "He especially liked to work with wood, so at the ranch he had a reserve store of cookstove wood all split and ready to carry in the house. About two or three years supply ahead. It was always a fascinating addition to the ranch and of great interest to our dudes." George moved to Jackson with Fred and Eva when they sold the ranch. After Fred died, Eva made sure that George was taken care of until he died.

Fred and Eva were very successful dude ranchers. For over forty years, hundreds of people came to the Moose Head Ranch to enjoy its homelike atmosphere and spectacular location. As Eva liked to say, "Our latch string was out to all who passed our way." Their guests came from all walks of life and hailed from countries like Sweden and Germany all the way to Africa and India. Their hunter guests ranged from the man who saved for years for one hunting trip with Fred to the mayor from California who hunted with Fred for twenty-five years.

At the end, they had forty log cabins and outbuildings, including a blacksmith shop and several cow barns for milking their twelve cows.

Top: George Greenwood and his famous woodpile, n.d. Jackson Hole Historical Society and Museum, 1958.3112.001. Bottom: With Fred Topping in front, dudes go out riding from the Moose Head Ranch, n.d. Jackson Hole Historical Society and Museum, 1958.0254.001

In the early days at the Moose Head Ranch, Eva cooked for as many as 60 guests a day. She is pictured here cooking in camp during a pack trip, n.d. Photo by Herb Pownall. Jackson Hole Historical Society and Museum, 1958.0253.001

Each summer they saw about sixty guests a day, and Eva finally hired a cook to help her out, even though she still did all the cooking in spring and fall. Successful as their business was, it remained hard work. And Fred and Eva were growing older.

In the fall of 1967, when Eva was was sixty-four years old and Fred was turning eighty-four, a man by the name of John Mettler was in Jackson Hole looking to buy a ranch. He had not found what he wanted and had a 1:00 p.m. flight out that day when his agent suggested that he take a look at the Moose Head Ranch. As the current Moose Head Ranch foreman and caretaker Dave Edmiston tells the story, "They went to look at it. As they drove up, Eva was butchering a beef, and Mr. Mettler introduced himself and they got to talking. She

Eva and Fred Topping serve the dudes at a Moose Head Ranch cookout, n.d. Jackson Hole Historical Society and Museum, 1958.0259.001.

said, 'I'm so tired. I can't do this work anymore. I want to sell the ranch.' Mr. Mettler asked what she wanted for the ranch, and she told him. He said, 'How about if I pay you so much down and pay the rest over 10 years?' She said okay right there in the barnyard, and he was on the plane at one o'clock that afternoon."

In late 1969, Eva and Fred moved into the house they had built in Jackson. Two months later, Fred died. He was eighty-six and had lived a colorful and versatile life as dude rancher, horseman, hunting guide, and entertainer. "He was a true lover of the great outdoors," Eva said of him, "with respect for animals, trees, flowers, anything in nature." Fred was also an active citizen in the Jackson Hole community. He served two terms as Teton County Commissioner and was a charter member of organizations like the Jackson Hole Chamber of Commerce, the Elks Lodge, and the Izaak Walton League, a conservation group. The pallbearers at his funeral included a large contingent of Jackson Hole old-timers, who were his friends.

Eva, now sixty-seven years old, continued to live life in her active mode. She became a charter member of the Business and Professional Women in Jackson. She served on the first board of directors of the Pioneer Homestead Apartments for Jackson Hole seniors. She was active with the Teton County Historical Society.

And she remarried. Bill Briggs, a widower from Tennessee whose children had grown up, had come to Jackson Hole. He had made friends with local families, and one day he walked by Eva's house in Cache Creek Canyon as she was working in her flower garden. She was nearing her seventieth birthday when she married him. Eva and Bill enjoyed Jackson's social life. After all her years of hard work, she had not forgotten how to have fun. "She liked to dance, and they liked to party and have a good time," said an old-timer from Mormon Row who also retired in town.

When she was eighty-four, Eva was named "Outstanding Woman in the Community" because of her years of community service. A year later, she died. "Valley Pioneer Dies," read the headline in the Jackson Hole newspaper obituary. Of her life with Fred as a homesteader and dude rancher, Eva said, "A lot of the oldtimers think that was a hard life for us. I never think about it that way. I think it was a beautiful life. I'd live it all over again. Running the dude ranch was a real adventure. It was the most wonderful challenge God ever put on earth."

The Moose Head Ranch lives on, in much the same style and atmosphere created by Eva and Fred. The Mettler family has fixed up some of the old log buildings and added some new buildings in a secluded spot below the original dude ranch. The ranch chef now lives in the cabin that was Eva's and Fred's home. Dave Edmiston has lived on the ranch for twenty-eight years and raised his family there. Year-round, he takes care of the ranch and of the fifty or sixty horses used

Eva Topping Briggs in her Jackson home in Cache Creek Canyon, 1983. Photo courtesy of Jackie Gilmore.

by the guests in the short summer season of ten weeks. In the winter, he still feeds moose along with the horses. Like Eva and Fred, the Mettlers do not advertise the Moose Head Ranch. And, as in Eva's and Fred's time, the ranch is usually booked solid ahead of time by the families who like to return every summer. It has been this way for sixty-seven years. And the view, as Eva exclaimed in 1927, is still "beautiful!"

The Jackson Hole homesteading era was relatively short. It started in 1884, and it closed in 1927, as Eva Topping found out to her dismay. In those forty-three years, a whole culture was started and took hold in Jackson Hole. It was based on hard work and on something else. Dave Edmiston put it well as he looked around the Moose Head Ranch: "It just fascinates me how these old timers came into this area, the hardships they faced, and the optimism they must have had."

Afterword

꠵━━◆━━○━━◆━━꠵

A S I wrote about the families in this book, I discovered that my own connection to them was stronger than just an author's connection to her work. I realized that my family's coming to Jackson Hole in 1956, and my life here, have taken me to places and to circumstances that connect me to the homesteaders. Like the Feuz family, for example, we were immigrants. We came from Denmark, one of the flattest countries on earth. Like Fred Feuz, my Father came to Jackson Hole, was enthralled by the mountains, and chose to stay. The family shared his feeling. My mother started mountaineering at the age of sixty-two. As with Geraldine Lucas at age fifty-nine, the first mountain she climbed was the Grand Teton. One of my favorite cross-country ski destinations is the porch of the Lucas cabin. Geraldine knew what she was doing when she picked that location for her home.

Old log cabins speak to me like no other buildings here. I agree with Struthers Burt of the Bar BC that "nothing is lovelier and fits more perfectly into the background from which it came than a Western log-cabin . . . . Its walls inside are restful to the eye, taking on a mellow ruddy patina as they get older. Moreover, they form the best of settings for anything you choose to put upon them. There is something of magic about the inevitable correctness of simplicity and usefulness."

For years, I have fondly lived and worked in historic log cabins.

I was the first desk clerk in Colter Bay Village. The cabin office where I worked was the old store from the Square G Ranch, and many of the guest cabins I rented out were also from the Square G. I had a honeymoon in a small log cabin on the shore of Jackson Lake in wonderful old Leek's Lodge, now sadly gone. Two of my favorite summers were spent on the Bar BC dude ranch in its declining years; yet even in its decline, it had the kind of atmosphere that lingers in one's memory and makes one smile.

For twelve years, I lived in Buster and Frances Estes's homestead cabin on the old STS dude ranch, now the Murie Ranch. Mardy Murie told me that when Buster and Frances built their cabin, all they had was $50 and a pregnant cow. For the $50, they built what was my kitchen. When the cow had a calf, they bartered and built what was my living room. I wrote a book on the ranch, made a film there, bought groceries at nearby Dornan's in Moose. Situated as it is in front of the Tetons and near the Snake River, the homestead cabin was my sanctuary—and also the best body builder I have ever known, with its winter-long demand for shoveling snow and chopping firewood.

My life with old log cabins continues. My office, in which I wrote this book, is a log cabin built in the early 1900s in Butler Creek, south of Wilson. It now stands in Cache Creek Canyon with a beautiful view up the canyon, where the sun rises and where clear sunsets bring alpenglow on distant mountains.

I choose to live in this valley because of its mountains and its community. I think many of the homesteaders had the same reasons. As Si Ferrin said about the mountains, "I've been looking at them for 46 years, but I've never known a moment when the Tetons didn't stir my soul." The community that the homesteaders built has left roots and values here that many of us locals respond to in our time: their independence, their self-reliance, their acceptance of diversity. And their ingenuity in doing whatever it took to make a go of it here. They helped each other whenever the need was there, and they saw this generosity as simply the way of being a neighbor and friend. They worked hard at what was meaningful to them. And, hard as that work surely was, they still gave time and energy to community, to education, to beauty, and to humor. I am grateful for the opportunity to write their stories.

Bonnie Kreps

SOURCE NOTES

꛰—◦—꛱

The Jackson Hole Historical Society and Museum, a major source of information for this book, will be referred to as JHHSM.

To check the homestead papers for homesteaders in this book, go to the Bureau of Land Management website: *www.glorecords.blm.gov/ PatentSearch/*.

Chapter One, The Shive Family

General background on the Shive family is collected from the following sources: The John Shive files at the JHHSM; Doris Platts, *John Cherry: His Lies, Life, and Legend*, page 44; Marion V. Allen, *Early Jackson Hole*, page 226; Orrin H. and Lorraine G. Bonney, *Bonney's Guide to Grand Teton National Park and Jackson's Hole*, page 44.

The memoirs by Lucy Shive's daughter and granddaughter can be found in: Frances Judge, "Carrie and the Grand Tetons," *Montana: The Magazine of Western History*, Summer 1968, pages 44–56; Frances Judge, "Vital Laughter," *Atlantic Monthly*, July 1954, pages 47–52; Frances Judge, "Second Life," *Atlantic Monthly*, November 1952, pages 58–62 (reprinted in *Montana Magazine of History*, Summer 1953, pages 20–26); and Frances Judge, "The Fun of Living!" *Naturalist*, volume 12, number 1, 1961, pages 9–15.

Carrie's description of her bed: "It had a marsh grass *tick*. . . ." The "tick" was the cloth case filled with marsh grass, wild clover, and mint that served as her firm, lower mattress.

Frances's description of Maw: "At sunup each morning Maw rose from the bed she had used more than one lifetime and built a fire. We children would be wakened by the scraping sound of the *lifter* moving over the stove as Maw, in her partial blindness, searched for the grooves that held the *lifter*." A "lifter" is the handle that could be hooked into the lid on a wood stove, so that the lid could be lifted off the stove to allow access to the firebox inside for starting or feeding the fire.

For more information on Jack Shive's climb of the Grand Teton, see Francis P. Farquahar, "Francis Spencer Spalding and the Ascent of the Grand Teton in 1898," *The American Alpine Journal*, volume 3, number 3, 1939, pages 302–309; and Reynold G. Jackson, "Park of the Matterhorns," in John Daugherty, *A Place Called Jackson Hole*, pages 274–275. The path followed by the party is known as the Owen-Spalding route and ascends the west face of the Grand Teton.

"Teams of horses would jog in from miles around, loaded with gay people, food and children, and dance all night to the swingy calls of Grandma Shive." See *Bonney's Guide*, page 44.

Chapter Two, The Hansen Family

Personal information about the lives of Peter and Sylvia Hansen comes from "Peter C. Hansen—Autobiography," pages 1–7, and "Sylvia I. Hansen—Autobiography," pages 1–19, on file at the JHHSM. Further information about the Hansen family comes from transcriptions of Cliff Hansen's two talks at the JHHSM, on 10/24/2001 and 12/14/2001; from his interview with Jo Anne Byrd, pages 1–27, for the JHHSM, 12/14/93; and from Parthenia Hansen Stinnett's oral history, pages 1–17, for the JHHSM, 6/16/83.

For more information about the way Peter Hansen built his diverse ranch holdings, his extra jobs, and the town of Jackson in 1914, see John Daugherty, *A Place Called Jackson Hole*, pages 172 and 206. Taking cattle to market over Teton Pass: (1) The Jimmy Brown ranch, started by Jim Boyles, was known as the Bar Y and was located adjacent to what is now Highway 22 near the intersection with Spring Gulch Road and west of the Emily Oliver place; (2) The Davis place was at the foot of Teton Pass and is now Trail Creek Ranch. For Cliff Hansen's political career, see T. A. Larson, *History of Wyoming*, pages 555–557.

For "Jackson Hole lost one of its best-beloved pioneers," see *Jackson Hole Guide*, 1/29/76, front page; "She was always helping people," see *Jackson Hole Guide*, 3/28/71, "Sylvia Hansen—A Proven Lady With Grit," page 7;

"What a wonderful life I have had," see *Jackson Hole News*, 1/19/76, "Sylvia Hansen—remembrances of a rich life," page 3.

Chapter Three, The Ferrin Family

For "If Jackson Hole ever had a cattle baron," see John Daugherty, *A Place Called Jackson Hole*, page 157; Si Ferrin as "Cattle King of Wyoming," see "Edith Ferrin Honored," *Jackson Hole News*, 2/4/71, page 15; Si Ferrin as "Uncle Si," see Marion V. Allen, *Early Jackson Hole*, page 207. For Merritt Ferrin's comments about his father throughout the chapter, see "An Interview with Merritt Ferrin" by Jay Brazelton for the JHHSM, 1973. For "I've been looking at them for 46 years," see "Gentleman Who Brought First Elk Out of Hole Still Sturdy," in the now defunct *Wyoming State Tribune* or *Wyoming Eagle*, volume 48, number 3, March, 1942. For "Here a major disappointment awaited" and the Si Ferrin plow story, see Fern K. Nelson, *This Was Jackson's Hole,* pages 199–201.

For Si's Twin Creek homestead, see John Daugherty, *A Place Called Jackson Hole*, page 128. For Si's "People from all over the Hole" and Si's helping to lay out the Jackson town site, see "Gentleman Who Brought First Elk Out of Hole," cited above. For Emmeline Ferrin's death, see *Jackson Hole Guide*, 12/6/79, page B17. For Edith Ferrin's handwritten memoir, see *Jackson Hole News*, 5/16/74, page 10. For Si getting his Buffalo Bench homestead, see *This Was Jackson's Hole*, pages 199 and 201.

For major facts about Si's building his landholdings, see John Daugherty, *A Place Called Jackson Hole*, pages 127,135, 137, 156–157, and 190. For the story of Si and the hungry elk, see *Bonney's Guide,* pages 106–107. For Si as community leader and game warden, see John Ryan, "Stories of Early Jackson People," April 1998, in the JHHSM files; also Marion V. Allen, *Early Jackson Hole*, page 212. For facts on the Ferrin ranch in its peak years, see "Edith Ferrin Honored," in *Jackson Hole News*, 2/4/71, page 15. For "largest outfit in Jackson Hole" and "times changed drastically," see John Daugherty, *A Place Called Jackson Hole*, pages 157 and 308. For "largest taxpayer in the county," see "Gentleman Who Brought First Elk Out of Hole Still Sturdy," cited above.

For the plight of Jackson Hole ranchers in the 1920s, see John Daugherty, *A Place Called Jackson Hole*, page 308, and David J. Saylor, *Jackson Hole, Wyoming: In the Shadow of the Tetons*, pages 171–172. For the reference to the role of John D. Rockefeller, Jr., in creating Grand Teton National Park, see John Daugherty, *A Place Called Jackson Hole*, page 9. For Si's selling his ranch and going bankrupt, see "Edith Ferrin Honored," *Jackson Hole News*, 2/4/71, page 15; *Bonney's Guide*, page 106, and Daugherty, *A Place Called Jackson Hole*, page 157. For Edith Ferrin's death, see "Grandma Ferrin Dies," *Jackson Hole Guide*, 5/16/74, page 18.

Chapter Four, The Burt Family

General background information about Struthers Burt can be found in the JHHSM biographical files and in the *Struthers Burt Papers* (C0039), Manuscripts Division, Department of Rare Books and Special Collections, Princeton University, on the web at *http://libweb.princeton.edu/libraries/firestone/rbsc/aids/burt-s.html*. Most information about Burt comes from his book *The Diary of a Dude-Wrangler*.

"I took one look and I've been here ever since," in "Jackson's Hole," a letter written to the editor of the *Jackson's Hole Courier*, 2/19/48, page 6; for Burt's uncle and great grandfather, see the same letter to the *Courier*, page 5. Burt at Princeton, German university, and Oxford: *Diary*, pages 13 and 15. "Financial Blue Beard" *Diary*, page 65; "an unrecorded wit" *Diary*, page 111; success of Bar BC, see Daugherty, *A Place Called Jackson Hole*, pages 221, 236, 362, and 233. "Almost every day we would get on our horses" and "We argued and fought endlessly," *Diary*, pages 87 and 93; "Western Bibles" and "from adzes to zithers," *Diary*, page 89; "we had to build a small town," *Diary* pages 88 and 90; Bar BC's first dude and twelve years later, and "That's the eighth typewriter," *A Place Called Jackson Hole*, pages 226–227, and *Diary*, pages 90 and 130–131.

Robert Betts quote, in Robert B. Betts, *Along the Ramparts of the Tetons*, page 160. "Hello, I'm a cavewoman," see Felicia Gizycka, "Cissy Patterson, The Countess of Flat Creek, by Her Daughter," in *Teton: The Magazine of Jackson Hole, Wyoming*, volume 10, 1977, page 40. Jack Huyler's story of Cissy Patterson is in his book *and That's the Way It Was in Jackson's Hole*, pages 109–110. Cissy and cussing story, *Along the Ramparts of the Tetons*, page 220. "Dude Ranches Out West," Union Pacific brochure ca. 1927. The cowboy as folk hero and dresser, *A Place Called Jackson Hole*, page 222, and *Diary*, page 50.

The dude ranch as "the single most unique contribution," *A Place Called Jackson Hole*, page 221; "grown like a mushroom in wet weather," *Diary*, page 48. The Bar BC cook: *Diary*, page 80; the Bar BC chief cowboy:

Diary, page 306. Struthers Burt writing successes, in *Struthers Burt Papers.* "The dude-wrangler is a . . ." *Diary*, page 57.

For the dude wrangler as conservationist, see Robert W. Righter, *Crucible for Conservation: The Struggle for Grand Teton National Park*, pages 11–12. "They were going to dam one of the near-by lakes," Struthers Burt quoted in *A Place Called Jackson Hole*, p. 175; "Here were threats," Margaret and Olaus Murie, *Wapiti Wilderness*, page 118; "This speedway down here," Struthers Burt quoted in *A Place Called Jackson Hole*, page 10; "You know, we were wrong," Struthers Burt quoted by Horace Albright in "Interview with Mr. Horace Albright by Assistant Superintendent of Grand Teton National Park Haraden and Chief Naturalist Dilley at Jackson Lake Lodge, September 12, 1967," page 13, historian's files, Grand Teton National Park. Robert Righter, "Preserving the Past: The Case of Grand Teton National Park," *Annals of Wyoming: The Wyoming History Journal,* Summer 1999, Volume 71, Number 3, page 11; "card parties, dinner parties," *Wapiti Wilderness*, page 121.

Robert Righter on meeting at Maud Noble's, *Crucible for Conservation*, page 33. Mr. Rockefeller and "quite the grandest and most spectacular mountains," in *Along the Ramparts of the Tetons*, page 198. Struthers Burt, "The Battle of Jackson's Hole," *The Nation*, March 3, 1926. Mr. Rockefeller gets impatient and "Jackson Hole Monument was now a fact," *A Place Called Jackson Hole*, pages 315–316. Cattle protest drive and Cliff Hansen's changing attitude, Cliff Hansen interview with Jo Anne Byrd, JHHSM, pages 11–13. For an in-depth report on the creation of Grand Teton National Park, see Robert W. Righter, *Crucible for Conservation: The Struggle for Grand Teton National Park.*

"On Saturday, Jackson Hole lost," *Jackson Hole Guide*, 9/2/54, front page; Katherine Burt memorial, "Memorial Service for Katherine Newlin Burt. Remarks by the Rev. Warren Ost. Chapel of Transfiguration, Moose, Wyoming, August 17, 1977," JHHSM files. Struthers Burt's "epitaph," *Diary*, page 28.

Chapter Five, The Feuz Family

General background on the Feuz family comes from Caroline Feuz Oliver, "The Family History of Fred Feuz and Caroline Durtschi Feuz, 1976," and from Linda Feuz Williams, "Feuz Family History," March 1, 2002. Both manuscripts are on file at the JHHSM. Caroline (Lena) is Fred and Caroline's daughter; Linda is their granddaughter. For information on Jackson Hole immigrants, see Daugherty, *A Place Called Jackson Hole*, page 104.

For "a lean-to to a lean-to" Williams, page 8; "We talked, we quarreled" Williams, page 11; "American Alps" Williams, page 18; "To the children it was wildly exciting" Oliver, page 4; "We woke up to find a new baby" Oliver, page 4; "It was work, work, work," Williams, page 25; "All summer long Mother irrigated," Williams, page 36; "Winter nights, I sewed," Williams, page 36; "They soon learned not to tangle with Grandpa," Williams, page 37; "Our horses were truly wonderful," Williams, page 25; "We got to be part of the family labor force" Williams, page 46; "God wanted it that way," Williams, page 64; "No matter how little money," Oliver, page 6; Feuz Christmas party, Williams, page 27; "Early in June, Father put me back of himself on his gentle saddle horse," Oliver, page 5; "Time passed," Oliver, page 6; Caroline "was one of the finest cooks he had ever known" and "they 'dined' by the light of a kerosene lantern," Williams, pages 37–38 and 26.

"In 1928 great changes came," Oliver, page 7; The Feuzes "still refused to sell," Williams, page 65; "*but we did what we could*," Williams, page 64; "After the painful decision" and "Father had a final heart attack," Oliver, page 7; "By his example he has shown all of us," see "Funeral Wednesday for Pioneer Resident," Fred Feuz obituary in JHHSM biographical files. "Mother was so eager," Oliver, page 8. In the Feuz family histories regarding Caroline Feuz Gertsch's departure from Jackson Hole, there are different views as to whether she, in fact, took her sewing machine. Caroline's daughter, Lena, recalled in 1976 that her mother left the little Singer sewing machine behind. Linda Feuz Williams, in her family history of 2002 noted that the old Singer had long been replaced and that her grandmother took her newer sewing machine with her to Midway. "It was a privilege, an absolute privilege," Williams, page 69; "Hope for the best," Williams, page 31; "The story of Fred and Caroline Feuz," Williams, page 1.

Chapter Six, The Chambers Family

For information about the Mormon Trail, go to "The Mormon Pioneer Trail" at *http://mormonpioneertrail.com/* and at *http://omaha.org/trails/* and "Mormon Pioneer" at *www.nps.gov/mopi/*.

For information about the Willie Handcart Company disaster, go to "Handcart Companies" at *http://historytogo.utah.gov/utah_chapters/pioneers_*

and_cowboys/handcartcompanies.html and "What happened to the Mormon handcart companies?" at *http://ldsfaq.byu.edu/view.asp?q=92*. For narrative and journal entries by members of the Willie Handcart Company disaster, go to *http://www.xmission.com/~nelsonb/handcart.htm* and *http://www.lds.org/ gospellibrary/pioneer/29_Rocky_Ridge.html*.

For background information about the Mormon Row community, which originally was known as Grovont, see Candy Vyvey Moulton, *Legacy of the Tetons: Homesteading in Jackson Hole*. For the story of George and Hanna May and their children, see *Legacy*, pages 44–45; for Thomas Alma Moulton and the Willie Handcart Company disaster, see *Legacy*, pages 47–54.

"You couldn't buy a job down there," in "Staking a Claim— Homesteading" 2/21/01, "Homesteading Stories" transcript, page 5, JHHSM; "One coyote hide was worth $25," Roy Chambers oral history, 3/4/88, page 2, JHHSM; "If you go from Moran to Jackson," in "Staking a Claim," 2/21/01, page 5, JHHSM; for general background information on Ida Chambers, see Ida Chambers interview with Jay Brazelton, 2/25/71, transcript of tape 051, JHHSM; "I was a real rookie schoolteacher," in "Mrs. Ida Chambers Named Cow-Belle of Year," *Jackson Hole Guide*, 5/6/71, page 6; "My Dad wouldn't give his consent," Ida Chambers interview, 2/25/71, pages 3–4, JHHSM; "She always said the thing that attracted her," Roy Chambers oral history, 3/4/88, pages 14–15; "The last time I ever wash a diaper," *Jackson Hole Guide*, 5/6/71, page 6; Ida Chambers as postmaster, *Legacy*, page 94, and Clark Moulton "Mormon Row History," page 3, JHHSM; "Everybody thought it was fun to stay at the Chambers,'" Roy Chambers oral history, 3/4/88, page 13, JHHSM.

Mormon Row irrigation, "Homesteading on Mormon Row, Roy Chambers," 7/11/2001, notes from a JHHSM history field trip, page 2; the fine art of dry farming, *A Place Called Jackson Hole*, pages 132–133; "90-day oat," Clark Moulton oral history, 5/13/83, page 3, JHHSM; "Even when I came along," in "Staking a Claim," 2/21/01, page 8, JHHSM; "You never did dare say you were bored," in "Staking a Claim," 2/21/01, page 11; "We got a really good education," in "Staking a Claim," page 15; "Recreation was the Saturday night dance," Clark Moulton, "Mormon Row History," page 3, JHHSM; "Our telephones were those long, box-like types," John Ryan, "Stories of Early Jackson People," April, 1998, pages 1–2, JHHSM.

Kelly flood background, *A Place Called Jackson Hole*, page 212; "But my Dad said, 'There isn't [any] danger'," Ida Chambers interview with Jay Brazelton, 2/25/71, pages 4–5; "The morning of May 18, 1927," J. R. Jones,

"Gros Ventre Flood," 5/21/27, pages 1–3, JHHSM; open water and "Miracle Spring," Cliff Hansen interview, 12/14/93, page 9, JHHSM.

"My mother kept kids," in Roy Chambers oral history, 3/4/88, page 13, JHHSM; "There were so many children," Roy Chambers oral history, 3/4/88, page 15, JHHSM; for Andy Chambers' death and Ida's continuing zest for life, see the family obituary for Ida, "Longtime resident Ida Chambers dead at 90," *Jackson Hole News*, 2/24/88, page 31; Anita Kathleen "Peach" Chambers 1936–1957, was the youngest of seven children of Andy and Ida Chambers. *Jackson Hole Guide*, 7/4/57 and Chambers Family Genealogy, JHHSM; "I've got a date downtown, Henry," in "Wyoming Outfitters Salutes Ida Chambers Francis," *Teton Magazine*, volume 4, 1981, page 24.

For the Andy Chambers Ranch listing in the National Register of Historic Places, see "The Andy Chambers Ranch Historic District" in "Grand Teton National Park National Register Properties," 6/29/98, historian's files, Grand Teton National Park, Moose, Wyoming; for general background information on the Michigan Volunteers, see Ed Brown, "Grand Tetons National Park: Michigan Volunteers," typescript manuscript, historian's files, Grand Teton National Park.

For local newspaper stories about the Michigan Volunteers, see "Row's Chambers place gets fixed up," *Jackson Hole News*, 10/11/95, page 11B; "A Conundrum at Mormon Row," *Jackson Hole News*, 7/3/96, page 7A; "Crandalls unearth past on Mormon Row," *Jackson Hole Guide*, 7/10/96, page 7A; "Partnership helps restore Mormon Row," *Jackson Hole Guide*, 7/10/96, page A6. "Some of those buildings were literally on the ground," in Margaret Foster, "Labor Not in Vain: Over and over, the Michigan Volunteers return to Wyoming to restore Mormon homesteads," 11/7/2003 at *http://www.nationaltrust.org/magazine/archives/arch_story/110703.htm*.

"This was the first year," in Ed Brown, "Grand Tetons National Park: Michigan Volunteers," page 2. "Without their work," in "Press Release: Michigan Volunteers and Lorna Miller Receive National Preservation Honor Award for Their Work on Grand Teton National Park, Wyo.," 10/2/03, at *http://www.nationaltrust.org/mountain_plains/newsletters/mpro-fall03.pdf*. For information about Moulton Ranch Cabins, go to *http:// www. moultonranchcabins.com/*.

Chapter Seven, Geraldine Lucas

For general background information about Geraldine Lucas, see Sherry

L. Smith, "A Woman's Life in the Teton Country: Geraldine L. Lucas," *Montana: The Magazine of Western History*, summer 1994, pages 18–33; Josephine C. Fabian, "The Lucas Place, 1914–1975," March 1, 1981, JHHSM files; and Bob Kranenberg interviews with the author, 2/19/04, 6/19/04, and 7/12/04, all in JHHSM files.

For Oberlin as the first college to admit both women and men, see Judith Hole and Ellen Levine, *Rebirth of Feminism*, page 2. Geraldine never spoke about her marriage, mentioned in Fern Nelson, *This Was Jackson's Hole*, page 271; Geraldine called her son Razz, in *This Was Jackson's Hole*, page 272. Geraldine and the Timber and Stone Act, in John Daugherty, *A Place Called Jackson Hole*, page 115, and Sherry L. Smith, "A Woman's Life in the Teton Country," pages 22–23. Her brothers' names were Lee and Woods. Her sister was Camilla. Geraldine "never failed to get a thrill," in Nellie H. VanDerveer, "A Pioneer's Last Rest: Geraldine A. Lucas," page 1, JHHSM files.

For information about women homesteaders and the popular literature about them, see Sherry L. Smith, "A Woman's Life in the Teton Country," page 25, and "Single Women Homesteaders: The Perplexing Case of Elinore Pruitt Stewart," *The Western Historical Quarterly*, May 1991, pages 163–183. See also Dee Garceau, *The Important Things of Life: Women, Work, and Family in Sweetwater County, Wyoming, 1880–1929*, pages 112–128.

Geraldine had a library of 1,350 books, and she "would sew until hell wouldn't have it, and she *never* wore a dress," see Sherry L. Smith, "A Woman's Life in the Teton Country," page 28; She valued these improvements at $7,000, "A Woman's Life in Teton Country," page 24.

For background information about Naomi Colwell, see Josephine C. Fabian, "The Lucas Place," manuscript, JHHSM files. Naomi sells her homestead to Geraldine for $500, see Warranty Deed #28006, Naomi Brewster Colwell to Geraldine A. Lucas, 5/19/1922, Teton County Clerk, Land Records office, Jackson, Wyoming; Naomi greeted as a returning heroine, "The Lucas Place," page 5.

"They said if you could work for Mrs. Lucas, you can work for anybody," and "She barked at the man," Bob Kranenberg interview with author, 6/19/04, pages 30–32, and 7/12/04, page 1.

"She had *lots* of courage," Quita Pownall interview with the author, 7/19/04, page l, JHHSM files. For the whole story of Geraldine's climb of the Grand Teton, see Paul Petzoldt, *Teton Tales*. "Mr. Owen said, 'Geraldine is very choosy,'" *Teton Tales*, page 17; she "asked me point blank," and "People just don't understand women like myself," *Teton Tales*, page 40; Geraldine on top of the Grand Teton, *Teton Tales*, pages 46–47.

Geraldine's 1936 letter to an Oberlin friend, "A Woman's Life in the Teton Country," page 32; Geraldine Lucas and John D. Rockefeller, Jr.'s Snake River Land Company, "A Woman's Life in Teton Country," pages 30–31, and *A Place Called Jackson Hole*, page 313; the Lucas place as an Oberlin summer school, "A Woman's Life. in Teton Country," page 32; Uncle Kimmel "had a great case on the little girl," in "The Lucas Place, 1914–1975," page 12; "Fabian, I can ruin your whole damn project," in "The Lucas Place," pages 7–8.

The Lucas place on the National Register of Historic Places, see Ann Hubber, "Geraldine Lucas Homestead/Fabian Place Historic District," National Register of Historic Places Nomination, Historian's files, Grand Teton National Park, 1997. "In that moment when she threw her arms around me with a soft sob," *Teton Tales*, page 47.

Chapter Eight, The Dornan Family

For Evelyn Middleton Dornan's ancestor, Arthur Middleton, and the Declaration of Independence, go to *http://wneclaw.wnec.edu/studentorgs/ PAD/Middleton.htm*.

"The way I heard the story," in "Bob Dornan on Evelyn Dornan and Family," interview with the author 7/30/04, page 2, JHHSM; "From time to time my father," and other Dornan family background, David Dornan and Reade Dornan, letters to the author, September 2004.

"I felt the urge to do War work," in "Diary of Evelyn Middleton Dornan," page 1, JHHSM; "I got $11.02 for my first week," *Diary*, page 2; "We finished the first women's wing," *Diary*, page 11; "Thursday, July 18, 1918. Bought my return ticket," *Diary*, page 12; "This morning I had my first horseback lesson," *Diary*, page 13; "I am surely having the time of my life," *Diary*, page 13; "Bought Peggy and her colt Kamal," *Diary*, page 18; "Got my homestead," *Diary*, page 23; "Gran was a strong, determined independent woman," in Dave Dornan, email message to author, September 18, 2004.

"There were no windows in the darn thing," in "Family History by Bob Dornan," 3/21/96, page 3, JHHSM; Jack Dornan's first winter in Jackson Hole, in Bob Dornan interview with author, 7/30/04, page 12, JHHSM, and "Homesteading Stories," 4/4/01, page 5, JHHSM; Gran "was rather a spoiled woman," in Bob Dornan interview with author, 7/30/04, pages 11–12,

JHHSM; "Jack why don't you," "Homesteading Stories," 4/4/01, page 5, JHHSM and Bob Dornan interview with author, 7/30/04, page 12, JHHSM.

For Evelyn Dornan's homestead testimony, see Department of the Interior Homestead Entry, U.S. Land Office, Evanston, Wyoming, No. 09075, Final Proof, Testimony of Claimant, Nov. 23, 1925, JHHSM. For Inspector C. S. Dietz's report, see United States Department of the Interior, General Land Office, FD 29013, Evanston, HE 09075, Favorable report, C. S. Dietz, November 24, 1926, JHHSM. "Evelyn got her land patent," see Department of the Interior, United States Land Office, Evanston, Wyoming, Serial No. 09075, Patent No. 999739, April 6, 1927, JHHSM.

"It was the start of the first commercial idea," in "Family History by Bob Dornan," 3/21/96, page 5, JHHSM; for background information about Joseph Reuben Jones, see *J. R. Jones, Preserving the Game: Gambling, Mining, Hunting, and Conservation in the Vanishing West.* "The Bet I Made With Uncle Sam," in *Preserving the Game,* page 95; "Education was extremely important," *Preserving the Game,* page 92.

"We Jones girls were educated," and "On week-ends, when weather permitted," and "Mrs. Estes was a debutante," and "Jack was to occupy most of the rest of my life," Ellen Jones Dornan oral history 10/6/82, pages 4–5, JHHSM; "He had a great personality," in "Family History by Bob Dornan," 3/21/96, pages 5–6, JHHSM; "It was a fight," Bob Dornan, personal comment to the author; "Dad was a great reader," Bob Dornan, interview with author, 7/30/04, pages 22–23, JHHSM; "We kids could pick some radio program," Bob Dornan, "Homesteading Stories," 4/4/01, page 23, JHHSM; "Every once in awhile," Bob Dornan, author interview, 7/30/04, pages 40–41, JHHSM.

"I'll never forget it!" and "Dad was really torn," culled from Bob Dornan, interview with author, 7/30/04, pages 23–24, JHHSM; Bonnie Kreps, "The Best Little Wine Shoppe Between Chicago and San Francisco," pages 97–98, *Jackson Hole News,* 12/20/78, page 18, and "Family History by Bob Dornan," 3/21/96, page 10. "This was when all the eastern dudes," in "The Best Little Wine Shoppe," page 98; "Dad never backed off from a fight," "Family History by Bob Dornan," pages 14–15, JHHSM.

"It has been observed that the Park" and "I think, mainly, it was a personal thing," Ellen Dornan oral history, 10/6/82, pages 8–9, JHHSM; "I'm still upset about it," Bob Dornan, interview with author, 7/30/04, page 26, JHHSM; "It always struck me as ironic," David Dornan in a letter to author, September 2004; "He was nosing around" and "He said, 'Mr. Dornan,' " culled from "Family History by Bob Dornan," page 15, and Bob Dornan, interview with author, pages 28–29, both JHHSM; "Yet, despite these negative memories," David Dornan letter to author; "He had a great deal of warmth" and "Jack was a character," Ellen Dornan oral history, 10/6/82, page 10 and pages 8–9, JHHSM; "Her spirit was indomitable," *Jackson Hole News* and *Jackson Hole Guide*, 4/11/01, page B11; "We deliver a good job to the tourists," Bob Dornan, interview with author, 7/30/04, page 29.

Chapter Nine, Albert and Lida Gabbey

General and personal background information about Albert and Lida Gabbey and the Square G Ranch comes from two interviews by the author with Tom and Ruth Lindley, Lida Gabbey's nephew and his wife. They worked on the Square G Ranch and have kept a family history. And from three interviews by the author with Bob Kranenberg, who was the Square G foreman and caretaker for many years. All the interviews are on file at the JHHSM.

The Square G Ranch was homesteaded, John Daugherty, *A Place Called Jackson Hole*, page 262; "tin-can tourists," the automobile revolution and Jackson Hole, and "Along the road," *A Place Called Jackson Hole*, pages 255–259; "the home of the Hollywood Cowboy," *A Place Called Jackson Hole*, page 10; guest ranches and dude ranches, Lindley interview, 9/20/04, page 8, and Bob Kranenberg, interview, 6/19/04, pages 7–8; "Mr. and Mrs. Square G," Lindley interview, 9/20/04, page 16. Gabbeys' Jenny Lake store rolled on logs to Square G, Bob Kranenberg interview, 2/19/04, page 12.

"We laid up the logs," and "I hauled all the water," culled from Bob Kranenberg interview, 2/19/04, pages 8–11 and 17; Square G brochure, 1934, courtesy of Bob Kranenberg; "I came to Jackson," Lindley interview, 9/20/04, pages 1 and 5–6, and Lindley interview 8/30/04, page 2; "I was only 18 years old," Lindley interview, 8/30/04, page 2; "My job started at 6 AM," Lindley interview, 8/30/04, page 13; "We saw the Square G grow," Lindley interview, 9/20/04, pages 7–8; "The Gabbeys were quite exceptional," culled from Lindley interviews, 8/30/04, page 8, and 9/20/04, pages 2–4; "He had a little old office," Kranenberg interviews, 6/19/04, page 21, and 2/19/04, page 14.

Albert Gabbey and the Land Office trouble, see *A Place Called Jackson Hole*, pages 118, 311, and 314, and Robert W. Righter, *Crucible for Conservation: The Struggle for Grand Teton National Park*, page 83. "Mr. Gabbey was a very strong, very fascinating, intelligent man," and Albert

Gabbey bear story, Ruth Lindley interview 8/30/04, page 6, and interview 9/20/04, page 10. "Did I tell you about the little four-year-old girl at the corral?" Bob Kranenberg interview, 6/19/04, page 12.

"The end of the dining room," and "They took great pride," Lindley interview, 9/20/04, pages 3–5 and 11; "This is one of the cabins," Kranenberg interview, 6/21/04, page 1; Lida Gabbey and Geraldine Lucas, Lindley interviews, 8/30/04, pages 14–16, and 9/20/04, page 11; death of Albert Gabbey, Lindley interview, 9/20/04, page 9, and *Jackson Hole Courier*, 10/2/47, page 1. "It was a big load for her," and "It was very sad and a big loss," Lindley interview, 9/20/04, page 9; "Log cabins, home-made lodgepole furniture," and "I have very warm memories," Rod Newcomb, letter to the author, 12/2/04.

Chapter Ten, Eva and Fred Topping

The interviews Eva Topping did with Jo Anne Byrd and Paul Knowles are all in the Topping files at JHHSM. "Women could homestead," interview by Jo Anne Byrd with Eva Topping, 7/1/83, page 4; "We children worked" and "We didn't have many cattle," Eva/Byrd interview 7/1/83, page 6; "When I was 13 years old," Eva/Byrd interview, 7/1/83, page 7; "I worked morning and night," Eva/Byrd interview, 7/1/83, page 8; "I applied to teach," Eva/Byrd interview, 7/1/83, page 9; "There were four eighth grade girls" and "The neighbors around there," Eva/Byrd interview, 7/1/83, page 11.

"They wanted the West real tough," Paul Knowles interview with Eva, 4/8/71, pages 1–2; "There was no machinery," Eva/Knowles interview, 4/8/71, pages 9–10; "When we started the Moose Head Ranch," Eva/Knowles interview, 4/8/71, page 15; "They just gave them away" and "They grew up with us," Eva/Knowles interview, 4/8/71, page 12; "I canned everything at the ranch," Eva/Knowles interview, 4/8/71, page 13; Eva and the Land Office problem, *A Place Called Jackson Hole*, pages 365 and 243; "From all evidence secured," see document, "Department of the Interior, United States Land Office, serial #015271, August 13, 1931," in JHHSM Topping file.

"The meat eaters" and "the hunters would come up," Eva/Byrd interview, 7/1/83, page 16; "Fred got the idea," Eva/Byrd interview, 7/1/83, page 17; Eva as postmaster, *A Place Called Jackson Hole*, page 137; "She had us up there," Dave Edmiston interview with the author, 8/20/04, page 1; "I had the tables set up" and "So I fed that gang," Eva/Byrd interview, 7/1/83, pages 21–23; "A letter from a New York City sportswriter," see letter with letterhead *The News, New York's Picture Newspaper*, 4/24/40, by Gene Ward, in JHHSM Topping file; Union Pacific brochure on Moose Head Ranch, *A Place Called Jackson Hole*, page 244; "We built 40 log cabins," Eva/Byrd interview, 7/1/83, page 16.

The Maytag family story, in "Teton County Has Colorful Past . . ." *Jackson Hole Guide*, 5/25/67, page 5. "Dear Fred" letter, see "Stone & Taylor" letter, 4/17/41, in JHHSM Topping file; "George was an excellent ax man," and "He especially liked to," Eva/Knowles interview, 4/8/71, page 13; "They went to look at it," Dave Edmiston in "Jackson Hole Journal" videotape #00/VT/04, JHHSM; "He was a true lover of the great outdoors," Eva/Knowles interview, 4/8/71, page 12; "She liked to dance," Marjorie Ryan interview with the author, 10/20/04, page 1, JHHSM.

Eva named "Outstanding Woman in the Community," *Jackson Hole News*, 7/7/88, page 29; "Valley Pioneer Dies," *Jackson Hole Guide*, 7/6/88, front page. "It just fascinates me," Dave Edmiston, interview with author, 8/20/04, page 3.

SELECT BIBLIOGRAPHY

><+>-०-<+>-<

Albright, Horace M. Interview by Robert C. Haraden and Willard E. Dilley, September 12, 1967. Transcript, Grand Teton National Park Library, Moose, WY.

Allen, Marion V. *Early Jackson Hole*. Redding, CA: Press Room Printing, 1981.

Armitage, Susan, and Elizabeth Jameson, eds. *The Women's West*. Norman and London: University of Oklahoma Press, 1987.

Basso, Matthew, Laura McCall, and Dee Garceau, eds. *Across the Great Divide: Cultures of Manhood in the American West*. New York and London: Routledge, 2001.

Betts, Robert B. *Along the Ramparts of the Tetons: The Saga of Jackson Hole, Wyoming*. Boulder, CO: Colorado Associated University Press, 1978.

Bonney, Orrin H., and Lorraine G. Bonney. *Bonney's Guide: Grand Teton National Park and Jackson's Hole*. Houston, TX: self-published, 1972.

Brown, Ed. "Grand Teton National Park: Michigan Volunteers." Typescript manuscript. Moose, WY: Grand Teton National Park Library, n.d.

Burt, Struthers. "The Battle of Jackson's Hole." *The Nation* 122 (March 3, 1926): 225–227.

Burt, Struthers. *The Diary of A Dude-Wrangler*. New York: Charles Scribner's Sons, 1924.

Daugherty, John. *A Place Called Jackson Hole: The Historic Resource Study of Grand Teton National Park*. Moose, WY: Grand Teton National Park, 1999.

Farquahar, Francis P. "Francis Spencer Spalding and the Ascent of the Grand Teton in 1898." *The American Alpine Journal* 3, no. 3 (1939): 302–309.

Garceau, Dee. *The Important Things of Life: Women, Work, and Family in Sweetwater County, Wyoming, 1880–1929*. Lincoln: University of Nebraska Press, 1997.

Gizycka, Felicia. "Cissy Patterson, The Countess of Flat Creek, by Her Daughter." *Teton: The Magazine of Jackson Hole, Wyoming* 10 (1977): 37–43.

Hole, Judith, and Ellen Levine. *Rebirth of Feminism.* New York: Quadrangle Books, 1971.

Huyler, Jack. *and That's the Way It Was in Jackson's Hole.* Second Edition. Jackson, WY: Jackson Hole Historical Society and Museum, 2003.

Jones, J.R. *Preserving the Game: Gambling, Mining, Hunting, and Conservation in the Vanishing West.* Compiled and co-edited by Reade W. Dornan. Boise, ID: Hemingway Western Studies Center, Boise State University, 1989.

Judge, Frances. "Carrie and the Grand Tetons." *Montana: The Magazine of Western History* (Summer 1968): 44–56.

Judge, Frances. "The Fun of Living!" *Naturalist* 12, no.1 (1961): 9–15.

Judge, Frances. "Second Life." *Atlantic Monthly* (November 1952): 58–62. Reprinted in *Montana Magazine of History* (Summer 1953): 20–28.

Judge, Frances. "Vital Laughter." *Atlantic Monthly* (July 1954): 47–52.

Kamma, Anne. *If You Were a Pioneer on the Prairie.* New York: Scholastic, Inc., 2003.

Kreps, Bonnie. "The Best Little Wine Shoppe Between Chicago and San Francisco." In *Jackson Hole: A Guide to History, Culture, and Recreation in the Valley*, 97–98. Jackson Hole, WY: First Light Ventures, Inc., n.d.

Larson, T. A. *History of Wyoming.* Second Edition. Lincoln, NE: University of Nebraska Press, 1990.

Limerick, Patricia. *Something in the Soil: Legacies and Reckonings in the New West.* New York: W. W. Norton & Company, 2000.

Limerick, Patricia, Clyde A. Milner II, and Charles E. Rankin, eds. *Trails: Toward a New Western History.* Lawrence, KS: University Press of Kansas, 1991.

Luchetti, Cathy. *Children of the West: Family Life on the Frontier.* New York: W. W. Norton & Company, 2001.

Moulton, Candy Vyvey. *Legacy of the Tetons: Homesteading in Jackson Hole.* Boise, ID: Tamarack Books, 1994.

Murie, Margaret, and Olaus Murie. *Wapiti Wilderness.* Boulder, CO: Colorado Associated University Press, 1985.

Nelson, Fern K. *This Was Jackson's Hole: Incidents and Profiles from the Settlement of Jackson Hole.* Glendo, WY: High Plains Press, 1994.

Painter, Nell Irvin. *Exodusters: Black Migration to Kansas after Reconstruction.* New York: W. W. Norton & Company, 1992.

Peavy, Linda, and Ursula Smith. *Frontier Children*. Norman, OK: University of Oklahoma Press, 1999.

Petzoldt, Paul. *Teton Tales*. Guilford, CT: The Globe Pequot Press, 1995.

Platts, Doris B. *John Cherry: His Lies, Life, and Legend*. Jackson, WY: Bearprint Press, 1991.

Righter, Robert W. *Crucible for Conservation: The Struggle for Grand Teton National Park*. Boulder, CO: Colorado Associated University Press, 1982.

Righter, Robert W. "Preserving the Past: The Case of Grand Teton National Park." *Annals of Wyoming: The Wyoming History Journal* 71, no. 3 (Summer 1999): 9–13.

Saylor, David J. *Jackson Hole, Wyoming: In the Shadow of the Tetons*. Norman, OK: University of Oklahoma Press, 1970.

Smith, Sherry L. "A Woman's Life in the Teton Country: Geraldine L. Lucas," *Montana: The Magazine of Western History* 44, no. 3 (Summer 1994): 18–33.

Smith, Sherry L. "Single Women Homesteaders: The Perplexing Case of Elinore Pruitt Stewart," *The Western Historical Quarterly* 22, no. 2 (May 1991): 163–183.

Werner, Emmy. *Pioneer Children on the Journey West*. San Francisco, CA: Westview Press, 1995.

West, Elliott. *Growing Up with the Country: Childhood on the Far Western Frontier*. Albuquerque, NM: University of New Mexico Press, 1989.

White, Richard. *"It's Your Misfortune and None of My Own": A New History of the American West*. Norman, OK: University of Oklahoma Press, 1991.

"Wyoming Outfitters Salutes Ida Chambers Francis." *Teton Magazine*, 4 (1981): 24.

INDEX

WE NEED YOUR FEEDBACK!

Dear Reader,

Please take a moment to tell us your thoughts on *Windows to the Past: Early Settlers in Jackson Hole*. Your comments will help us to improve our publications program in the future. (Please note that the targeted readership for this book is a general audience.)

READER SURVEY

Disagree . . . . **Agree**

The book connected me to the people, events, and places that characterized Jackson Hole in the early days.

1	2	3	4	5

The book furthered my knowledge and understanding of the early settlement of Jackson Hole, including the challenges and rewards of the people that settled the valley.

1	2	3	4	5

The book increased my curiosity about the history of:

My hometown   1   2   3   4   5

My family   1   2   3   4   5

What were the book's strengths?

_____

_____

_____

_____

How could the book have been improved?

_____

_____

_____

_____

_____

_____

_____

_____

_____

_____

Did the book engage you? How? Why or Why not?

_____

_____

_____

_____

_____

_____

_____

_____

_____

Please mail your comments to:
Jackson Hole Historical Society and Museum
P. O. Box 1005, Jackson, WY 83001
Or, visit our website to complete this form.
www.jacksonholehistory.org
Thank you.

Jackson Hole
Historical Society
& Museum

The Jackson Hole Historical Society and Museum is a not-for-profit organization devoted to the collection and study of local and regional history. Its mission is heritage education. In the late 1980s the museum, founded in 1958, and the historical society, begun in 1965, merged to form the organization we have today.

To support its mission, the historical society and museum offers a wide variety of educational programs, from walking tours of historic downtown Jackson, to history excursions and book discussion groups, to customized programs for local and regional students, as well as wide-ranging historical exhibits. The organization also publishes scholarly works on the history of the region. These activities help local residents and visitors to the area understand its western heritage and reflect on the future of the community.

In addition to a permanent artifact collection, the historical society and museum features a research library with archival and biographical data, maps, oral histories, and photograph archives. The collections showcase cultural materials from prehistoric times, the story of the fur trade, and the presence of Native Americans. They also explore the lives of the people that settled the valley, how they used the land and natural resources, and the traditions and culture that they developed.

The Jackson Hole Historical Society and Museum is a 501(c)(3) charitable organization. For more information about the historical society and museum, please call (307) 733-9605 or visit the website at:

www.jacksonholehistory.org.

OTHER TITLES

published by the Jackson Hole Historical Society and Museum

Please check with your local bookseller, or order the following publications directly from JHHSM by using the form at the back of this book, or by visiting the Jackson Hole Historical Society and Museum website at: www.jacksonholehistory.org

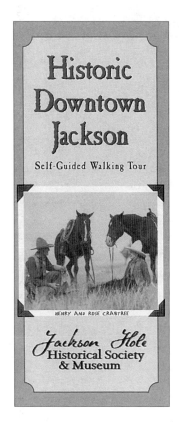

Historic Downtown Jackson: A Self-Guided Walking Tour

The Jackson Hole Historical Society and Museum invites you to step back in time and imagine Jackson's remarkable history through a self-guided walking tour of the town's historic buildings. This informative brochure contains a map and description of 20 locations accessible within a single, easy walking tour. The entertaining commentary and wealth of historic photos, along with recommendations of other historic sites to visit throughout the valley, make this publication a "don't miss" for anyone curious about the early days of Jackson Hole.

Jackson Hole: Crossroads of the Western Fur Trade, 1807–1840
by Merrill J. Mattes

Merrill J. Matte's study of the origin of whites in Jackson Hole was born during the controversy that raged over creation of Jackson Hole National Monument. The monument lay adjacent and to the east of then small, mountainous Grand Teton National Park. It included Jackson Lake and the Snake River, and extended east to the Gros Ventre Range that forms the eastern boundary of Jackson Hole. Monument opponents saw it as a step toward expansion of the park, and maintained that nothing historically significant had occurred in Jackson Hole to warrant such designation, a requirement for monument status. Mattes was asked to rebut that contention and he made his case in the research that forms the basis of this book: That Jackson Hole had a recorded human history and an importance; that it was a crossroads of the fur trade in the sense that it was a corridor for travel between South Pass and such destinations as the Yellowstone and Big Horn basins, the headwaters of the Missouri, and the Pacific Northwest coast; and that nearly every expedition of consequence between the years 1807 and 1840 passed through the valley, while some individuals, notably David Jackson, stayed to trap. *Jackson Hole: Crossroads of the Western Fur Trade, 1807–1840* is an engrossing read.

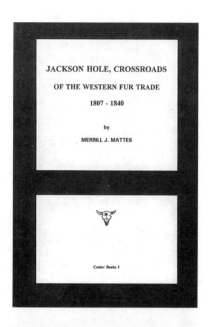

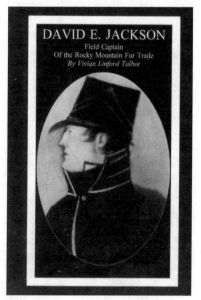

David E. Jackson, Field Captain of the Rocky Mountain Fur Trade
by Vivian Linford Talbot

Vivian Linford Talbot's excellent biography of David E. Jackson tells the captivating story of the mountain man

whose fame lives on in the lake, town and valley that bear his name. Jackson fought Native Americans, avoided grizzly bears and endured the rigors of the wild to become one of the most successful trappers of his time.

Landmarks of the Rocky Mountain Fur Trade: Two One-Day Self-Guided Tours from Jackson, Wyoming
by Pierce Olson

With this authoritative, comprehensive and, above all, fascinating guidebook, readers can easily visit the places where fur trade history was born, and visualize the people and events that gave human importance to the surrounding canyons, mountains and valleys. Author Pierce Olson received his B.A. and M.A. degrees in history at Stanford University, and served five years on the Board of Directors of the Jackson Hole Historical Society and Museum, including two years as Board President.

and That's the Way It Was in Jackson's Hole
by Jack Huyler

Publications Award 2001, Wyoming State Historical Society
Certificate of Commendation 2005, American Association of State and Local History

Jack Huyler's award-winning *and That's the Way It Was in Jackson's Hole* features engaging stories of Jackson Hole from the Huylers' arrival in 1926 until the present. Within the book's pages you'll meet pioneers, a gunman, horse traders, ranchers, dude ranchers and a mule man. You'll visit Jackson's bars during prohibition and the "joints" where illegal gambling flourished. You will read of murder, cabin fever, dance halls, dances, and of the last time the town of Jackson was "shot up." "Tall Tales, Most of them True" will tickle your imagination, and the inside information of rodeos, dude ranches and Grand Teton National Park is invaluable. Jack Huyler's wonderful stories are enhanced by the inclusion of over 70 historic photos.

Historic Photographs also available for sale.
Visit the Jackson Hole Historical Society and Museum's website at:

www.jacksonholehistory.org

Notes

Order Form

To order additional copies of Windows to the Past or other JHHSM publications, please check with your favorite bookseller, or send a copy of this form with your personal check or money order to:

Jackson Hole Historical Society and Museum
P. O. Box 1005 • Jackson, Wyoming 83001

Qty.	Price ea.	Publication Title	Total
____	$16.95	Windows to the Past: Early Settlers in Jackson Hole	_____
____	$3.95	Historic Downtown Jackson: A Self-Guided Walking Tour	_____
____	$7.95	Jackson Hole, Crossroads of the Western Fur Trade	_____
____	$7.95	David E. Jackson, Field Captain of the Rocky Mountain Fur Trade	_____
____	$11.95	Landmarks of the Rocky Mountain Fur Trade	_____
____	$18.95	and That's the Way It Was in Jackson's Hole	_____
		Subtotal	_____
		Wyoming residents add 6% sales tax	_____
		Shipping $2.50 per publication	_____
		Grand Total	_____

Please enter the address you wish to send this order to:

Name _____

Mailing Address _____

City/State/Zip _____

Phone number _____